THE ACCOUNTS OF ALPHONSE OF POITIERS, 1243-1248

A Quantitative Edition

Francis X. Hartigan
University of Nevada, Reno

UNIVERSITY
PRESS OF
AMERICA

LANHAM • NEW YORK • LONDON

University Press of America,™ Inc.

4720 Boston Way
Lanham, MD 20706

3 Henrietta Street
London WC2E 8LU England

Printed in the United States of America

ISBN (Perfect): 0-8191-4228-X
ISBN   (Cloth): 0-8191-4227-1

cc

All University Press of America books are produced on acid-free
paper which exceeds the minimum standards set by the National
Historical Publications and Records Commission.

306189

For Rachel and Peter

ACKNOWLEDGEMENTS

I am especially grateful to Eleanor Roach for her
efforts to see this project completed. A study of the
accounts was begun by Miss Roach's brother as a Ph.D.
dissertation but it was not completed. The project was
called to my attention by Professor John Bell Henneman
then at the University of Iowa and I agreed to under-
take it. The success of this project is to be shared
with these people; I am alone responsible for its
shortcomings.

Thanks are due to my colleagues in the History
Department for their encourgement and to the members of
the Western Society for French History for their help-
ful advice.

The Research Advisory Board of the University of
Nevada, Reno provided a summer stipend to facilitate
work on the project.

My wife, Judith Ellis Hartigan, gave valuable
assistance in the preparation of the manuscript.

TABLE OF CONTENTS

The Accounts of Alphonse of Poitiers...........page 1

Notes...page 16

Table of Accounting Terms.......................page 19

All Saints' Day, 1243...........................page 20

Candlemas, 1243.................................page 28

Ascension, 1244.................................page 35

All Saints' Day, 1244...........................page 42

Candlemas, 1244.................................page 49

Ascension, 1245.................................page 54

All Saints' Day, 1245...........................page 62

Candlemas, 1245.................................page 69

Ascension, 1246.................................page 75

All Saints' Day, 1246...........................page 81

Candlemas, 1246.................................page 88

Ascension, 1247.................................page 96

All Saints' Day, 1247...........................page 104

Candlemas, 1247.................................page 110

Ascension, 1248.................................page 117

All Saints' Day, 1248...........................page 124

THE ACCOUNTS

OF

ALPHONSE OF POITIERS

Quantification is one of the most important research methods used by historians. Fundamental to the
effective use of it is the availability of accurate
data. Without accurate data historical quantification
is doomed to yield false results and may actually im-
pair our understanding of the past. It is the inten-
tion of this work to provide accurate data for quantitative analysis of one of the most important sources
for the history of thirteenth-century France, the accounts of Alphonse of Poitiers.

Quantification has had its detractors. Carl
Bridenbaugh in his 1962 presidential address to the
American Historical Association warned historians to
shun "that Bitch-goddess, QUANTIFICATION."[1] Now an important debate rages among historians about the value
and role of quantitative history. While it is not our
purpose to review this debate in detail, it is worth-
while to indicate the direction of the debate and to
survey some of the pertinent issues. Lawrence Stone
observes that quantification may no longer captivate
historians. He maintains that there is today a revival of narrative history fueled by the recognition
that history is a complex discipline and that a story -
the narrative - rests at the heart of all historical
enterprise.[2]

Discussing narrative history and quantitative history, Bernard Bailyn in his 1981 American Historical
Association presidential address, "The Challenge of
Modern Historiography," argued that writing "essential
narratives...(is)...the great challenge of modern historical scholarship."[3] While Bailyn worries about the
excesses of technical studies, he does find in quantitative history a new range of inquiry which he calls
"latent events." These are "events that contemporaries
were not fully or clearly aware of," such as subtle,
long-term, economic and population changes.[4]

David Herlihy, who is well known for his use of
quantitative history and for his advocacy of quantitative methods, has stated the case for modern quantitative history most effectively when he argues "that
both the enthusiasm which greeted computational methods

in the late 1950s and 1960s, and the present skepticism concerning their use, were and are exaggerated."[5] Essentially Herlihy calls for a mature, knowledgeable approach to quantification, an approach which recognizes that quantification and the computer are powerful and flexible tools for use by historians, but tools only. Herlihy, then, has no quarrel whatsoever with narrative history; but rather believes that it can be enhanced by quantitative methods. On the other side of the issue, he is particularly hard on the cliometricians whom he accuses of too limited a use of formal analysis and a lack of rigor in collecting and criticizing their information. As for quantification itself, Herlihy finds it an old interest of historians which goes back at least to the eighteenth century and one that has yielded much knowledge and will continue to do so for a long time to come.[6]

It must be remembered by those who use quantification and by those who reject it, that it is in itself only a method, not an end. As a method it has incontestably enriched our knowledge of the past. Its value is multi-faceted: it adds precision to historical analysis, it is largely free from some of the judgmental problems affecting other forms of evidence, it allows historians to extract more illusive evidence from appropriate documents than literary analysis alone permits, and - perhaps most important - it opens to historians the world of illiterate people whose historical tracts may be found only in such records as tax roles, censuses, manorial obligations, monastic charters, and other mundane, numerical documents. If quantification does not always help us to see the individual, it does provide us with the collective experience of past generations, classes, families, and regions. Many fields of historical inquiry would be crippled without the quantitative method; demography and prosopography, financial and institutional history, economic and social history are among the fields which benefit from this methodology.[7] Indeed, quantification is one of the best methods for uncovering Bailyn's "latent events" of history.

Quantitative history begins with accurate data. Historians, like miners, must find and extract ore, then refine and process it into concentrate. Only then is it ready for the forge of formal analysis by history's craftsmen. The present volume seeks to provide an accurate edition - the concentrate - of the numerical evidence contained in one important medieval financial document. It does not draw conclusions, it does not craft the final product, but it does correct serious problems and near fatal mistakes in the nineteenth-century edition of the accounts of Alphonse of Poitiers. As part of the refining process it organizes the evidence for immediate use by historians who may wish to do homage to the "bitch-goddess," use it to add weight to their narratives, help uncover latent events, or explore it in its own right as a rich mine of information about thirteenth-century France and England. The document in question - the accounts of Alphonse of Poitiers for the years 1243 to 1248 - is preserved in the Archives Nationales in Paris (series KK, number 376). The need for a quantitative edition of this document arises from the fact that the existing edition by A. Bardonnet is seriously flawed as far as quantitative evidence is concerned.[8]

Quantitative evidence is so scarce for the Middle Ages that accurate recording of what does exist is of the utmost importance for medievalists. This is especially true for the accounts of Alphonse of Poitiers. The accounts are unique because they represent one of the best records of French financial administration for the thirteenth century and because they cover an unbroken period of more than five years, a remarkably long period for medieval sources. Alphonse's accounts were arranged in three accounting terms per year, so we have in KK 376 sixteen consecutive terms. This consistency and continuity is unmatched by any other financial record of the period.

The weakness of Bardonnet's edition is that he carelessly recorded the numerical entries. Quantitative evidence was not as important in the nineteenth century as it is now, but the errors in Bardonnet are so numerous that use of the edition yields unreliable results. It is now known that nineteenth-century editors often ignored or discounted evidence in the documents they edited, discarding valuable ore among the tailings. K. F. Werner has demonstrated that many nineteenth-century editors were careless about properly recording mundane information such as witness lists from charters. Thanks to Werner's efforts to obtain accurate witness lists by returning to the original manuscripts, the structure of Carolingian aristocracy is better known and standard views about the aristocracy are greatly changed.[9] The work of Werner and this present volume suggest that historians must return to the original manuscripts in cases where numerical and other mundane information is critical for historical analysis. It may prove necessary for historians to produce new quantitative editions of medieval documents containing numerical information. From what we know now, historians should not extract quantitative information from older editions without checking the accuracy of the edition against the original manuscript. This is particularly true because information once discarded as low grade ore is not profitably mined through the technique of quantification.

Because the purpose of this volume is to correct the errors of Bardonnet by returning to the original manuscript and to prepare the accounts for quantitative analysis by arranging the contents of each of the accounting terms in chart form, it is hoped that this work will remove the accounts from the obscurity that has enveloped them, expose this rich vein of historical information, and provide a concentrate ready for historical fabrication. After all, the accounts have much to offer as sources for French and Anglo-French history as well as for the history of medieval society, economics, warfare, feudalism, etc. Moreover, a sound edition of the accounts is the last task necessary to provide complete and competent sources for a much needed modern study of Alphonse of Poitiers and his role in the affairs of the period.[10]

Before we examine the accounts themselves we must say a few words about Poitou and historical events there in the thirteenth century. The accounts are the financial record of the administration of Poitou from 1243 to 1248. These years fit snugly and significantly between Alphonse's military success in controlling Poitou and his departure to join his brother, Louis IX, in the Seventh Crusade.[11]

The county of Poitou served as a borderland between northern France and Aquitaine to the south. In the Middle Ages it was known to the English as an unruly place. It was they who had controlled it - or tried to - since the establishment of the Angevin Empire through the marriage in 1152 of Henry of Anjou and Eleanor of Aquitaine, who as countess of Poitou and duchess of Aquitaine was the heir of the house of Poitou which had ruled the county since 902.[12] The English considered the Poitevin a particularly treacherous creature.[13] The French, too, distrusted Poitevins; Louis VII distrusted those in the entourage of Eleanor of

Aquitaine during the Second Crusade.[14]

Despite the attitudes of those who would rule it, Poitou was important to both the English and French monarchies. A glance at its physical and political geography will explain why. The most important geographical feature of medieval Poitou is the "Seuil du Poitou." This plain of Poitou has considerable historical significance because it serves, like the neck of an hour-glass, as the connection between the Loire Valley to the north - with the large and wealthy Parisian basin beyond it - and, to the southwest, the important basin of Aquitaine. The plain of Poitou is the easiest, the most direct, indeed the natural passage between northern and southwestern France and beyond that, Spain. The plain, however, is crowded on the east and west by highland regions which force it into a relatively narrow passage known to geologists as the "Détroit du Poitou," the straits of Poitou.[15] In the straits is found Poitiers, the principal city of the province. Located astride this major route, Poitiers is a meeting ground between southern and northern France. Because of its location the city has considerable military advantages and consequently became an important battle ground. In 507 Clovis and his Franks defeated the Arian Visigoth Alaric II at nearby Vouillé, thus driving the Visigoths out of Gaul and into Spain. From Spain the Arabs attacked across the Pyrenees and in 732 drove northward until they were stopped by Charles Martel in a battle fought between Poitiers and Tours, a battle long considered one of history's most decisive engagements. Almost equally famous and equally decisive was the battle of Poitiers fought in 1356 in which England's Black Prince not only crushed the French but also captured King John the Good, his youngest son Philip, and his pride of French nobility. This battle of Poitiers ended the first phase of the Hundred Years' War.

These famous battles are only the highlights among innumerable conflicts that swept across medieval Poitou. In the first half of the thirteenth century conflict between England and France for control of Poitou was particularly sharp and especially important. English leadership in this period was as poor as that of France was good. England was led for much of the century by the durable but inept Henry III (1207-1272, king 1216-1272), while France prospered under the leadership of the long-lived Louis IX (1214-1270, king 1226-1270). The English gained a role in Poitevin affairs when

5

Henry of Anjou, husband of Poitou's countess Eleanor of Aquitaine, became king of England as Henry II. The sons of Henry and Eleanor proved far less able than their father. Angevin kingship was weakened by Magna Carta (1215) and the disastrous reign of John Lackland (1199-1216). John's son Henry III enjoyed one of England's longest though least successful reigns.

John and his son Henry found disaster in Poitou. Perhaps John's folly was never greater than when in 1200 he absconded with Isabelle of Angoulême, the betrothed of Hugh of Lusignan, who was count of La Marche and head of the powerful Lusignan family of Poitou. This offense to one of the major families of the region was a serious political mistake.[16] Hugh vainly sought compensation from John and only after many months did he turn to his and John's ultimate lord, the king of France. Philip Augustus (1180-1223) could not have had a better excuse to turn his nominal suzerainty into actual seizure and control of Angevin land.[17] He carefully exploited his legal position over all Angevin lands in France, but for territorial agrandizement he concentrated on a single target: Normandy. Poitou would have to wait. Philip completed his conquest of Normandy in 1204. The loss of Normandy to the French monarchy was a devastating blow to the Angevin continental empire. Moreover, Philip had set the stage for the recovery of other provinces, including Poitou. When Philip died in 1223 Poitou was not yet under French control, but his son Louis VII, although he reigned only three years (1223-1226), found the time and energy to conquer Poitou (1224) and Languedoc, thus further spliting Angevin lands north from south in the case of Poitou and, in the case of Languedoc, placing the Capetians along the eastern flank of English Aquitaine. His son Louis IX - St. Louis - began his reign as a minor under the regency of his mother, Blanche of Castile, and ruled in his own right from 1234 to his death in 1270. Although the regency was a time of trouble for the Capetians, later Louis IX was more than a match for his adversary Henry III.

Henry III came to the throne at age nine in 1216 and began to rule in his own right in 1232. He launched a major effort to recover Poitou in 1230. The campaign, which ended in 1231, was unsuccessful and Henry returned to England poorer for his efforts.[18] His next major attempt came in 1242 which brings us directly to the accounts of Alphonse of Poitiers. Alphonse was the fourth son of Louis VII and Blanche of Castile and one

6

of four of their twelve children to survive adolescence. Queen Blanche arranged for her youngest surviving son to marry Jeanne of Toulouse, the nine-year-old daughter and heir of count Raymond VII of Toulouse. According to the terms of the agreement Toulouse and all that pertained to it was to go to Alphonse or his heirs by Jeanne; if the couple were to die childless Toulouse would pass to the crown.[19] It is of the utmost significance for the development of the French monarchy that Alphonse and Jeanne, who inherited her father's lands after his death in 1249, in fact did die without issue (21 and 24 August 1271, respectively), thus passing Toulouse and Poitou directly to the crown. Alphonse had received Poitou and Auvergne from his father as an apanage, a region ruled by a younger son in co-ordination with the monarchy.[20] Alphonse was to co-ordinate his rule of Poitou and Auvergne, and the inheritance of his wife, with that of France by his eldest brother Louis IX.

When Alphonse went to take possession of Poitou in 1241 he found himself faced with serious problems. Not only did the English oppose his rule, but opposition to him developed among the Poitevin barons as well. This opposition was led by Hugh of Lusignan, count of La Manche, and his wife Isabelle of Angoulême, widow of John Lackland and mother of Henry III. Hugh was the son of Isabelle's original financé from whom she was taken by John. Isabelle's sons by Hugh, half-brothers to her son Henry III, wanted to involve Henry in Poitevin affairs. Relations between England and the Lusignan family were close.[21] At the Christmas court in Poitiers Hugh started the rebellion against the Capetians by refusing to do homage to Alphonse and by burning the house in which Alphonse was staying in Poitiers.[22] Alphonse appealed for aid to Louis IX; Hugh appealed to Henry III. Henry invaded Poitou from Gascony but was soundly defeated at Taillebourg and therefore abandoned the war in Poitou.[23] However, he did not recognize the loss of Poitou until the treaty of Paris in 1258.[24] Charles Petit-Dutaillis called the period from 1152 to the treaty of Paris "the First Hundred Years' War."[25] French success in Poitou marked a definite stage in the long conflict between England and France that characterized the medieval and early modern history of the two nations. It was after the victories in 1242 that Alphonse began the systematic recording of his financial affairs in Poitou that survive as the accounts that bear his name. He continued these records until he left for the crusade in 1248.

7

The accounts represent Alphonse's efforts to organize the newly acquired area so that he could go on a crusade leaving behind a well-ordered and profitable estate.

The subject of this present volume is the register containing the accounts rendered to count Alphonse of Poitiers by his administrative officers (baillis) from All Saints' Day term, 1243 to All Saints' Day term 1248. Sixteen accounting terms - three per year - span this period. The manuscript is the oldest of four thirteenth century financial records from France which are written on paper.[26] Paper was used perhaps as a cheaper substitute for parchment for records considered routine and mundane. It is their very routine and mundane nature, as well as their duration, that make the accounts so valuable to historians.

The register is the original manuscript and is the product of several scribes. It is relatively clear and legible, with few interlineations, marginalia, or strikeouts, especially remarkable for a financial document. The manuscript contains several lists having nothing to do with the accounting records themselves. It begins with such lists and they are often inserted between accounting terms where the scribes left blank leaves. For example, between Ascension, 1244, and All Saints' Day, 1244, there is a list of the liegemen of the count of Poitiers written in a hand different from that which wrote the accounts for the Ascension term. Following this list the same scribe who had written the Ascension term resumed again with the All Saints' Day accounts.[27] The manuscript was considered a good place to record information of value to the count even though it had nothing to do with the accounts themselves. The additions, which normally are undated, may have been placed in the manuscript well after the original accounts were written. For our purposes in this volume we consider the insertions tailings and exclude them from the processed ore. Some of the insertions are written in French; the accounts themselves are always in Latin.

The insertions aside, the sixteen accounting terms were written by three scribes, whose hands appear in succession without overlapping:

SCRIBE	TERMS	NUMBER OF TERMS
A	All Saints' Day, 1243- Candlemas, 1244	5
B	Ascension, 1245 to folio 87r, entry Expensa	1
C	Ascension, 1245 from the Expensa entry through All Saints' Day, 1248	10

The manuscript itself is generally well preserved
but there was some damage to it. Due to the porous
quality of the paper smearing was a problem. Frequently
the scribes struck out illegiable words and rewrote them
either above the line or farther along it. A few pas-
sages were damaged through deterioration of the paper
and the vicissitudes of time. Defective entries are
not included in the tables.

The manuscript consists of 163 numbered folios
measuring 175mm by 130mm. The first four gatherings
vary in size from four to ten leaves. Beginning with
the fifth gathering which starts on folio 55, the manuscript is divided into gatherings of eight leaves each,
except for the last one, which has six leaves. Generally the margins are narrow except where the scribes were
forced to work around defects in the paper. Scribe A,
for example, used generous spacing and few abbrevia-
tions, whereas Scribe C crowded his lines together in
an effort to get as much as possible on the page.

The accounts have little in common with modern
financial records for a number of reasons. Systematic
recording keeping was not common to the Middle Ages.[28]
Receipts and expenses, although they are kept separate,
were normally recorded without attention to any
particular order. Often the scribes simply made entries
as they occured, but some development of a more organized structure can be seen across the sixteen terms.
In the first four terms the balli did not attempt a
classification of receipts but simply wrote down each
item individually. Then in the fifth term, Candlemas,
1244, there is an important organizational change. The
balli began to classify receipts according to their
source. This improvement not only made the accounts
more useful to Alphonse, but also to the modern his-
torian. Entries were not recorded in tabular form as
one might expect from exposure to modern financial

documents. Instead, the information is recorded in
prose-like paragraph form. The numbers, therefore, are
not arranged in columns. This style, coupled with the
problems inherent in working with Roman numerals,
created problems for the scribes themselves who often
made errors in adding the figures together. In the present edition the figures are arranged in columns. The
manuscript was written before the invention of double-
entry bookkeeping so totals also were written in prose
style. Besides the errors in addition, the scribes
made errors of omission and substraction.

The register was published by A. Bardonnet in the
Archives historiques du Poitou, IV (1875). Bardonnet
did not carefully record the numerical entries. Because the true value of the manuscript is in the
numerical data it contains, Bardonnet's inaccuracies
make his edition misleading and unsuitable for modern
quantitative analysis. Accurately transcribing the
often confusing Roman numerals, especially those
written indistinctly by hasty scribes, is no easy task.
But Bardonnet mistranscribed numerals even when they
were plainly written. Most of Bardonnet's errors
involve only small sums but occasionally his mistakes
involved large sums of money. For example, the entry
for total relief payments for All Saints' Day, 1246,
was recorded by Bardonnet as 19 librae[29] though the
manuscript plainly states 1900 librae.[30] In this
instance the scribe wrote: XIX^C. The use of a superscript for tens, hundreds, and thousands is routine in
this manuscript and any editor should have been familiar
with the practice from the very first accounting term.
Bardonnet simply ignored the clearly written superscript
thereby introducing an enormous error. His works suf-
fers too from errors of omission. He failed to record,
for example, any reference to profits from the forest
of Moulière for All Saints' Day, 1247, although the
entry is clearly written in the manuscript.[31] In the
Ascension term, 1248 he neglected to mention revenue
from the provostship of Benon.[32] Major errors such as
these, as well as innumerable smaller ones, destroy
the value of Bardonnet's edition of the accounts of
Alphonse. The tables in the present edition are based
upon the manuscript and all entries are in Arabic
numerals.

The scribes, as mentioned above, distinguished between receipts and expenses. Provostships, or smaller
revenue districts, were usually farmed out on an annual
basis with payment due in each of three terms per year.

The lease for the farm went to the highest bidder. It
was the successful bidder's task to raise enough to meet
his payments and have a profit for himself. Tax farm
payments were usually entered as "pro primo tercio,"
"pro secundo tercio," and "pro ultimo tercio." On oc-
casion one finds irregularities in the way farms were
reported. For example, all three payments for the farm-
ing of Poitiers in 1244 were recorded as "pro primo
tercio." Perhaps the farm was relet three times that
year, but that is unlikely because the payments (100
librae) neither rise or fall. Perhaps the scribe himself was confused and simply repeated the first payment
designation. Most of the major farmed revenues were
consistent in the way they were recorded. When the term
for a tax farm was ended, the farm was relet, sometimes
at higher payments. The major sources of revenue were
usually kept continuously farmed. The major non-farmed
revenues, such as wood sales or large reliefs, produced
important revenues often at regular intervals. In the
fifth term, Candlemas, 1244, the revenue was recorded,
as we have noted, according to its source. The bailli
used two important categories for receipts: the Domain
of the Count and the Domain of Hugh de La Marche. The
first of these refers to the lands directly under the
count and the second is the domain of Hugh of Lusignan
which the victorious Alphonse confiscated. The original
domain of the count was itself enlarged by forfeitures
after the defeat of Hugh and Henry III. The income from
the count's domain is remarkably steady throughout the
period covered by the register. The consistency of the
receipts is primarily due to the fact that the provostships for the five major towns in the domain - Poitiers,
La Rochelle, Saint-Jean-d'Angély, Niort, and Benon -
were tax farmed. These five were farmed for as little
as 130 librae per year for Saint-Jean-d'Angély to as
much as 1600 librae per year for La Rochelle. The annual farms were paid in three equal installments, so
the accounts show little variation over time. In three
instances, however, the provostships were not farmed:
La Rochelle for All Saints' Day, 1243, and Poitiers, for
Candlemas and Ascension, 1248. The amount of the farms
changed only slightly except for that of La Rochelle
which dropped from 1600 librae per year to 1500 librae
in 1248, the last year of our record. Normally the
revenues from these towns accounted for about two-
thirds of the total revenue for the domain of the count.

Other revenue from the domain included rents on
those dwelling in the forest and from the sale of forest
products. Revenue from sales was usually paid in five

11

or six installments over a period of two or three years.
Sales from the forest were designated simply as "venda
foreste" without further elaboration. It is perhaps
safe to assume that these were timber sales because
land sales in the forest usually contain reference to
the units (arpents) of land sold. The number of
arpents was mentioned at each payment. Forest sales
were spread across the sixteen accounting terms in such
a way as to provide a fairly dependable source of revenue over the period covered by our records.

A variety of smaller revenue sources are found in
the accounts for the domain of the count: small
reliefs, rents, legal actions, and so on. There is an
assessment of the Jews of Saint-Jean-d'Angély at Candlemas, 1243 and Candlemas, 1244, each time for 40
librae.[33]

The second domain, that of Hugh de La Manche,
which had come under the control of Alphonse of Poitiers
through forfeiture, was larger than the count's original
domain. Receipts from it were greater than those from
the original comital domain in all but two accounting
terms (Ascension, 1246 and Candlemas, 1246). The La
Marche domain contained fewer town provostships than
the comital domain, but its largest single farm, Aunis,
rivals La Rochelle in total revenue. The revenues for
"the grand fief of Aunis," as it is called in the
manuscript, rose from 1150 librae in the first year to
1301 librae in the last. Unlike La Rochelle the Aunis
tax farm represented revenue from a large rural region.
The number and kind of the entries for the La Marche
domain also indicate its rural nature. The revenues,
moreover, were comparatively small for the Candlemas
and Ascension terms, while All Saints' Day, which is
after the harvest, produced the largest sums. On this
last point the urban character of the original domain
of the count is attested to by the evenness of the revenues throughout the year. The original domain produced a steady and reliable income. The remaining tax
farms in the domain of Hugh de La Marche were much
smaller than that of Aunis.

Expenses occasioned little difficulty for the
bailli or the scribes because they tended to organize
themselves under relatively few headings: castle garrisons, alms, money fiefs, and repair work. Expenses,
then, are consistently arranged from the beginning of
the accounting terms.

The money òf account used in the register was the royal _livre_ _tournois_ (_libra_ _turonensium_). Frequently the scribes added the word "turon(ensium)" after the monetary entries, especially in the earlier accounting terms. In time the scribes took it for granted that the _livre_ _tournois_ was understood as the money of account, the descriptive term "turon(ensium)" is used less and less. While the money of account was the _livre_ _tournois_ this does not mean that sums mentioned in the text were necessarily collected in that currency. Alphonse struck his own coins, which, at least at the time of this register, were the same in weight and alloy as the royal _livre_ _tournois_.[34] Occasionally the scribes mentioned the _livre_ _poitevin_, Alphonse's coin. The _bailli_ received coins of both types, as the following entry from Candlemas, 1246 indicates: "...in custodia pro domino comite IIII^M V^C libr. pictavensium, et per nos in Templo magistro Reginaldo, XII^C XVI libr. XVII sol. X den. turon."[35] An arrearage of 5807 _librae_, 9 _solidi_, 1 _denarius_ in Ascension, 1247 was paid 3000 in _livres_ _poitevins_ and 2807 _libr._, 9 _sol._, 1 _den._ in _livres_ _tournois_.[36] The balance for that same Ascension term was recorded as "tam pictavensium quam turonensium."[37]

   In the tables sums are given under the headings "libr.," "sol.," and "den." (_libra_, _solidus_, _denarius_ respectively). I have avoided the conventional English symbols for pounds, shillings, and pence so that confusion will not arise between pounds sterling and thirteenth-century French money. There are 12 _denarii_ to a _solidus_ and 20 _solidi_ to a _libra_.

   We have already noted that the accounts of Alphonse of Poitiers were organized into sixteen accounting terms beginning with the All Saints' Day term of 1243 and ending with the All Saints' Day term of 1248. There were three accounting terms per year: Candlemas, celebrated February 2; Ascension, the fortieth day after Easter; and All Saints' Day, November 1. These terms are not uniform in the number of days because Candlemas term, containing 93 days, was shorter than the other two. Ascension normally consisted of 135 days except for Leap Year, which occured in 1244 and 1248, when it consisted of 136 days. There were 137 days in each All Saints' Day term. The figures in the accounts reflect the different lengths of the terms.

   The year in thirteenth-century France began at Easter, a fact that Alphonse and his officials wisely

13

chose to ignore. Because Easter is a moveable feast,
the "year" in France could vary from 330 to 400 days,
from 11 to 13 months.[38] Giry observed, for example,
that the "year 1236," according to Easter style for the
beginning of the year, began on March 30, 1236 and ended
on April 18, 1237.[39] By using three accounting terms
none of which began or ended at Easter, Alphonse escaped
the confusion inherent in the Easter style. Ascension
too is a moveable feast but the term it represented was
fixed. The term periods were Candlemas, November 9 to
February 9; Ascension, February 10 to June 24; All
Saints' Day, June 25 to November 8. Confusion is pos-
silbe, however, especially for the Candlemas term which
according to the Easter system falls at the end of the
year, but is the first term in the year according to the
modern style of January 1. In the manuscript the first
Candlemas term occurs in 1243, according to the Easter
system, but according to the modern style, called "New
Style," it would be 1244. The following table shows
this difference:

YEAR (Easter Style)	TERMS	DAYS IN TERM	YEAR (New Style)
1243	All Saints' Day	137	1243
	Candlemas	93	1244
1244	Ascension	136	
	All Saints' Day	137	
	Candlemas	93	1245
1245	Ascension	135	
	All Saints' Day	137	
	Candlemas	93	1246
1246	Ascension	135	
	All Saints' Day	137	
	Candlemas	93	1247
1247	Ascension	135	
	All Saints' Day	137	
	Candlemas	93	1248
1248	Ascension	136	
	All Saints' Day	137	

     There are five tables of each accounting term.
The first table is the "Summary Account: Original
Manuscript Totals." This table contains the numerical
information as it is recorded in the manuscript. The

second table is the "Summary Account: Reorganized
Totals." This table contains information from the
manuscript but it is organized in a different manner.
As we have noted, the bailli changed from a random recording of receipts in the first four accounting terms
to one based upon the source of the revenue. The
"Reorganized Totals" carry this change backward to the
first four terms so that analysis of revenues across
the sixteen terms may be more easily made. In addition
this table is useful to historians who seek specific
information on expenditures for alms, salt profits,
grain sales, etc. Slight variations occur in the
figures in the "Original Manuscript Totals" and in the
"Reorganized Totals" primarily due to incorrect addition
by the scribes whose totals (given in the "Original
Manuscript Totals") may actually not be the correct sum
of the entries. Also, the scribes from time-to-time
omitted mention of some of the items that went into
making their totals. Such omissions, of course, can
not be included in the "Reorganized Totals." Refine
our ore as we might, perfect purity is not obtainable.
The third and fourth tables break down information for
the important domains of the count of Poitou and Hugh
de La Marche. The last table is that of garrison
expenses which were the most important expenses listed
in the accounts. Where appropriate there are additional
tables for garrison payments in forfeited lands, summary account of the royal fund in Poitou, and accounts
independent of the control of the bailli.

NOTES

[1] Carl Bridenbaugh, "The Great Mutation," American Historical Review, LXVIII (1963), p. 326. See also J. Morgan Kousser, "Quantitative Social-Science History," The Past Before Us, ed. Michael Kammer (Ithaca, 1980), p. 434.

[2] Lawrence Stone, "The Revival of Narrative: Reflections on a New Old History," Past and Present, 85 (1979), pp. 3-24.

[3] Bernard Bailyn, "The Challenge of Modern Historiography," American Historical Review, LXXXVII (1982), p. 7.

[4] Bailyn, p. 10.

[5] David Herlihy, "Numerical and Formal Analysis in European History," Journal of Interdisciplinary History, 12 (1981), pp. 115-116.

[6] Herlihy, 132-135.

[7] Among the many good essays on quantitative methodology see Francois Furet, "Quantitative History" in Felix Gilbert and Stephen R. Graubard (eds.), Historical Studies Today, (New York, 1972), pp. 45-61 and J. Morgan Kousser, pp. 433-456.

[8] A. Bardonnet, Comptes d'Alphonse de Poitiers (Poitiers, 1875), IV, Archives historiques du Poitou.

[9] Karl Ferdinand Werner, "Unterschungen zur Frühgeschichte des Französischen Fürstentums," Die Welt als Geschichte (1958): 256-289; (1959): 146-193; (1960): 87-119. See also his introduction to administrative history "Histoire comparée de l'administration," pp. ix-xxxiv in Histoire comparée de l'administration (IVe-XVIIIe siècles), (Munich, 1980).

[10] The accounts have not been widely used. See Bélisaire Ledain, Histoire d'Alphonse, frère de Saint Louis, et du comté de Poitou sous son administration, 1241-1271, (Poitiers, 1869); Edgard Boutaric, Saint Louis et Alfonse de Poitiers, (Paris, 1870); A. Bardonnet, Comtes d'Alphonse de Poitiers (Poitiers, 1875); Thomas N. Bisson, "Negotiations for Taxes under Alfonse of Poitiers," XIIe Congrès international des sciences historiques. Etudes présentées à la commission internationale pour l'histoire des assemblées d'états (1966), pp. 77-101; G. Nahon, "Les Juifs dans les domaines d'Alphonse de Poitiers, 1241-1271," Revue des études juives, CXXV (1966), pp. 167-211; Francis X. Hartigan, "The Financial Administration of Alphonse of Poitiers, 1243-1248: Reunification and Stability," Proceedings of the Sixth Annual Meeting of the Western Society for French History, VI (1979), pp. 2-9. It must be remembered that the accounts concern Poitou alone. Secondary sources and documents for his administration elsewhere exist in reliable editions. See Auguste Molinier, Etude sur l'administration féodale dans le Languedoc (900-1250),

(Toulouse, 1878); Etude sur l'administration de Saint Louis et d'Alphonse de Poitiers dans le Languedoc, (Toulouse, 1880); and Alphonse de Poitiers: Mandements inédits, (Toulouse, 1900). To work of Molinier must be added the contribution of Pierre-Francois Fournier and Pascal Guebin, Enquêtes administratives d'Alfonse de Poitiers: Arrêts de son parlement tenu à Toulouse et textes annexes, 1249-1271, (Paris, 1959). Also very useful is A. Teulet et al., Layettes du Trésor des chartes, 5 vols. (Paris, 1863-1909). The work of these scholars together with this quantitative edition of the accounts now make possible a modern study of Alphonse of Poitiers.

[11] Joinville, The Life of Saint Louis (Baltimore, 1963), pp. 209-210. For the role of Alphonse in the crusading efforts of Louis IX see William Chester Jordan, Louis IX and the Challenge of the Crusade (Princeton, 1979). Alphonse died after participating in Louis's unsuccessful Tunis crusade. Jordan, p. 214.

[12] For Eleanor and her family see Alfred Richard, Histoire des comtes de Poitou, 778-1204 (Poitiers, 1903).

[13] See Matthew Paris, Chronica Majora, IV, pp. 205, 210-211, 216, 221-222. See also Antonia Gransden, Historical Writing in England c.550-c.1307 (London, 1974), pp. 356-379, 404-438.

[14] Amy Kelly, Eleanor of Aquitaine and the Four Kings (London, 1952), pp. 14, 54, 56, 79, 170-171.

[15] Jules Welsch, Les régions naturelles de Poitou dans les départments des Deux-Sèvres et de la Vienne (Paris, 1927), p. 9.

[16] Robert Fawtier, The Capetian Kings of France: Monarchy and Nation, 987-1328 (New York, 1966), pp. 146-147. Sidney Painter has studied the Lusignan family in three important articles: "Houses of Lusignan and Châtellerault, 1150-1250," Speculum, XXX (1955), pp. 374-384; "Castellans of the Plain of Poitou in the Eleventh and Twelfth Centuries," Speculum, XXXI (1956), pp. 243-257; "The Lords of Lusignan in the Eleventh and Twelfth Centuries," Speculum, XXXII (1957), pp. 27-47. See too Harold Snellgrove, The Lusignans in England, 1247-1258 (Albuquerque, N.M., 1950).

[17] On the Capetian dynasty see Fawtier.

[18] For a brief discussion of the reign of Henry III see Bryce Lyon, A Constitutional and Legal History of Medieval England (New York, 1980), pp. 337-345. Also see Matthew Paris, Chronica Majora, IV.

[19] Bélaisaire Ledain, pp. 2-3; Fawtier, pp. 134-125.

[20] On the concept and importance of apanage see Charles T. Wood, The French Apanages and the Capetian Monarchy, 1224-1328 (Cambridge, 1966).

[21] The Metropolitan Museum of Art (New York) possesses in its Cloisters Collection a jewel box from this period with a cover which blends the English royal arms with that of the House of Lusignan. See also Matthew Paris, IV.

[22] Edgard Boutaric, p. 53 and Ledain, p. 18. Matthew Paris, IV, pp. 178-179.

[23] Matthew Paris, IV, pp. 209-212. Joinville, pp. 188-189.

[24] The treaty was concluded 28 May 1258 but not published until 4 December 1259. Therefore some confusion has resulted as to the year of the treaty. See Charles Petit-Dutaillis, The Feudal Monarchy in France and England from the Tenth to the Thirteenth Century (London, 1936), p. 227; Fawtier, p. 152; Boutaric, pp. 54-57; Ledain, pp. 21-27; and Michel Gavrilovitch, Etude sur le traité de Paris de 1259 (Paris, 1899).

[25] Petit-Dutaillis, p. 230.

[26] Maurice Prou, Manuel de paléographie latine et francaise (Paris, 1924), p. 33.

[27] Archives Nationales (Paris), KK 376, folios 54-59.

[28] All medieval records are in their way unique. Such well-known records as Domesday Book and the so-called budget of the French monarchy (Ferdinand Lot and Robert Fawtier, Le premier budget de la monarchie française, 1202-1203 (Paris, 1932) have strong internal peculiarities and fall far short of modern standards of record keeping.

[29] Bardonnet, p. 135. See below note 35.

[30] KK 376, 111.

[31] KK 376, 132v; Bardonnet, p. 175; see below p. 106, item 14.

[32] KK 376, 143r; Bardonnet, p. 198; see below p. 128, item 3.

[33] See below p. 32, item 9 and p. 51, item 10.

[34] J. Lecointre-Dupont, "Essai sur les monnaies de Poitou et sur leurs divers types," Mémoires de la Société des Antiquaires de l'Ouest, VI (1840), pp. 358-360, and Edgard Boutaric, "Histoire monetaire d'Alfonse, comte de Poitiers et de Toulouse," Revue Numismatique, 13 (1868), pp. 285-287.

[35] KK 376, 123 and Bardonnet, p. 159.

[36] KK 376, 125, 129 and Bardonnet, p. 162 and 171.

[37] KK 376, 130 and Bardonnet, p. 171.

[38] A. Giry, Manuel de Diplomatique (Paris, 1893), p. 110.

[39] Giry, p. 110.

TABLE OF ACCOUNTING TERMS

Number	Term	Manuscript Folio	Bardonnet Page
1.	All Saints' Day, 1243	26r	23
2.	Candlemas, 1243	38r	37
3.	Ascension, 1244	48r	48
4.	All Saints' Day, 1244	60r	65
5.	Candlemas, 1244	77r	81
6.	Ascension, 1245	83r	90
7.	All Saints' Day, 1245	88r	99
8.	Candlemas, 1245	97r	112
9.	Ascension, 1246	104r	123
10.	All Saints' Day, 1246	110r	133
11.	Candlemas, 1246	117r	147
12.	Ascension, 1247	125r	162
13.	All Saints' Day, 1247	131r	173
14.	Candlemas, 1247	138r	186
15.	Ascension, 1248	143r	197
16.	All Saints' Day, 1248	152r	215

ALL SAINTS' DAY, 1243

SUMMARY ACCOUNT OF THE GENERAL FUND:

ORIGINAL MANUSCRIPT TOTALS

Item	Subtotal			Total		
	l.	s.	d.	l.	s.	d.

Receipts:

		l.	s.	d.	l.	s.	d.
1.	Payment by the castellan of Niort	2125	9	0			
2.	Debt of Harduin de Malle	1718	0	0			
3.	Sales of grain	583	16	5			
4.	Sales of wine	276	16	6			
5.	Bailliage of Poitiers	882	12	6			
6.	Forfeited lands at Saint-Maixent	145	8	4			
7.	Bailliage of Niort	546	9	4			
8.	Bailliage of Benon[1]	234	9	7			
9.	Bailliage of Aunis	884	10	9			
10.	Forfeited lands in Aunis	334	1	9			
11.	Bailliage of Saint-Jean d'Angély	203	15	6			
12.	Bailliage of Saintes	534	17	6			
13.	Forfeited lands at Saintes	319	0	8			
14.	Profits of justice	500	0	0			
	TOTAL RECEIPTS:				9289	7	10

Receipts separated and repeated:[2]

		l.	s.	d.	l.	s.	d.
1.	Payment by the castellan of Niort	2125	9	0			
2.	Debt of Harduin de Malle	1718	0	0			
3.	Sales of grain	583	16	5			
4.	Sales of wine	276	16	6			
	TOTAL:				4704	1	11
	REMAINING RECEIPTS:[3]				4585	5	11
	MANUSCRIPT BALANCE:[4]				4585	6	0

Expenses:

1.	Garrison payments	1407	2	1	
2.	Alms and feudal dues	645	0	0	
3.	Public works[5]	167	12	0	
4.	Wages of the <u>bailli</u>	164	0	0	

```
          TOTAL:                              2383 14  1
          MANUSCRIPT TOTAL:                   2383 14  1

BALANCE DUE TO THE COUNT:[6]                  2201 11 10
MANUSCRIPT BALANCE:[7]                        2201 12  0
```

[1] This entry is the sum of the individual items because no total is given in the manuscript.

[2] These entries represent items carried forward from previous accounting terms and extraordinary sources of income. Why the <u>bailli</u> chose to substract "receipts separated and repeated" from total receipts is not readily discernable although such procedure did permit the separation of extraordinary and ordinary sources of revenue. The procedure is abandoned by the <u>bailli</u> between Candlemas, 1244 and Ascension, 1246.

[3] This figure is the remainder when the separated and repeated receipts are substracted from the total receipts.

[4] The manuscript balance has a discrepancy of one <u>denarius</u>.

[5] This entry is the sum of the individual items because no total is given in the manuscript. Such editorial calculations are no longer noted in the tables.

[6] The <u>bailli</u> arrived at this figure by substracting expenses from "remaining receipts" and not directly from total receipts.

[7] The manuscript errs by two <u>denarii</u>.

SUMMARY ACCOUNT OF THE GENERAL FUND:

REORGANIZED TOTALS

Item	Subtotal			Total		
	l.	s.	d.	l.	s.	d.

Receipts:

1. Domain receipts:
   - A. Domain of Count Alphonse

A. Domain of Count Alphonse	1319	18	3			
B. Domain of Hugh de La Marche	1267	18	5			
TOTAL DOMAIN RECEIPTS:				2587	16	8
2. Payment by the castellan of Niort				2125	9	0
3. Debt of Harduin de Malle				1718	0	0
4. Sales of grain				583	16	5
5. Sales of wine				276	16	6
6. Profits from the salt beds				23	19	0
7. Sales of salt at Saintes				178	14	6
8. Diverse receipts:						
A. Forfeited lands	1265	6	10			
B. Minor reliefs	20	0	0			
C. Aids and sale of hay at Saintes	8	10	0			
D. Profits of justice	500	0	0			
TOTAL DIVERSE RECEIPTS:				1793	16	10
TOTAL RECEIPTS:				9288	8	11

Expenses:

1. Garrison payments				1407	2	1
2. Alms and feudal dues:						
A. Feudal dues	574	3	4			
B. Alms	70	16	8			
TOTAL:				645	0	0
3. Public works				167	12	0
4. Wages of the _bailli_				164	0	0
TOTAL EXPENSES:				2383	14	1

BALANCE DUE TO THE COUNT:[2]				6904	14	10
MANUSCRIPT BALANCE:				6904	13	11

[1]The reorganized total is 18s., 11d. less than the original manuscript total. This difference arises from differences among the figures themselves.

[2]This figure is substantially different than that of "the balance due to the count" in the original manuscript total primarily because the "receipts separated and repeated" are not subtracted from receipts in the reorganized totals.

ALL SAINTES' DAY, 1243

DOMAIN OF THE COUNT OF POITIERS

Item	Revenue		
	l.	s.	d.
1. Provostship of Poitiers	100	0	0
2. Profits from the forest of Moulière	12	2	0
3. Sale of wood in the forest of Moulière	183	6	8
4. Provostship of Niort	106	13	4
5. Revenues from Benon	20	6	3
6. Aids from Boece	60	0	0
7. Provostship of Benon	76	13	4
8. Aids at Anais	5	0	0
9. Sale of wood in the forest of Benon	62	10	0
10. Profits from the forest of Benon	10	0	0
11. Provostship of La Rochelle (before farming out)	640	0	0
12. Provostship of Saint-Jean-d'Angély	43	6	8
TOTAL:	1319	18	3

ALL SAINTS' DAY, 1243

DOMAIN OF COUNT HUGH DE LA MARCHE

Item	Revenue		
	l.	s.	d.
1. Land of Count Hugh de La Marche at Poitiers (before farming out)	19	4	0
2. Farm from the land of Count Hugh at Poitiers	72	10	0
3. Provostship of Montreuil	103	6	8
4. Sale of wood in the forest of Montreuil	70	0	0
5. Sale of dead wood at Saint-Hilaire	5	0	0
6. Provostships of Niort, Prahecq, and Coulons (before farming out)	33	7	8
7. Provostships of Frontenay, Coulons, and Prahecq	146	13	4
8. Farm of Cherveux	33	6	8
9. Rents at Sanxay	5	5	6
10. Legal pleas at Frontenay	6	0	0
11. Minor legal pleas at Prahecq	7	19	0
12. Sale of wine at Prahecq	5	13	0
13. Minor legal pleas at Cherveux	5	10	0
14. Provostship of Tonnay-Boutonne	40	0	0
15. Provostship of Tonnay-Boutonne (before farming out)	6	10	9
16. Grand fief of Aunis (before farming out)	31	5	6
17. Aids of Lissieuil and Marsill in the fief of Aunis	100	0	0
18. Aids of Chauzay in the fief of Aunis	66	0	0
19. Minor rents in Aunis		14	6
20. Fief of La Croix-Comtesse	26	13	4
21. Receipts from the bailliage of Saintes while Jean de l'Ile held it	15	19	0
22. Provostship of Saintes (before farming out)	30	0	0
23. Provostship of Saintes	128	6	8
24. Fief of Ramegot	11	6	0
25. River dues at Saint-Jean-d'Angély (before farming out)	2	14	3
26. River dues at Saint-Jean-d'Angély	3	6	8
27. Aid at Saint-Jean-d'Angély		12	2
28. Aids from the abbess of Saintes at the feast of St. Michael	175	0	0
29. Aids of Saint-Anais at the feast of St. John	7	0	0

30.	Aids of Saint-Anais at the feast of St. Michael	50 0 0
31.	Relief of hospitality at Château-Neuf	6 12 0
32.	Relief of hispitality at Saint-Gemme	4 5 0
33.	Relief of hospitality at La Vergne	1 1 6
34.	Relief of hispitality at Favaux	5 16 0
35.	Sale of wine at La Verge	3 9 3
36.	River dues in the woods of Affre	1 10 0
37.	Sale of wood in the forest of Baconais	30 0 0
38.	Profits from the forest of Baconais	6 0 0
	TOTAL:	1267 18 5

ALL SAINTS' DAY, 1243

GARRISON PAYMENTS

(TERM: 137 DAYS)

Item	Per Diem			Total		
	l.	s.	d.	l.	s.	d.
1. Poitiers	1	2	8	155	5	4
2. Saint-Maixent		19	7	134	2	11
3. Niort	2	7	2	323	1	10
4. Benon	1	0	10	142	14	2
5. La Rochelle	3	4	4	440	13	8
6. Saint-Jean-d'Angély		10	5	71	7	1
7. Surgeres	1	0	5	139	17	1
TOTALS:	10	5	5	1407	2	1
MANUSCRIPT TOTAL:				1407	2	1

CANDLEMAS, 1243

SUMMARY ACCOUNT OF THE GENERAL FUND:

ORIGINAL MANUSCRIPT TOTALS

Item	Subtotal			Total		
	l.	s.	d.	l.	s.	d.

Receipts:

1.	Arrearage from Harduin de Malle	100	0	0			
2.	Debt of the castellan of Saint-Maixent	33	6	8			
3.	Bailliage of Poitiers	580	9	5			
4.	Bailliage of Niort and Saint-Maixent	509	9	7			
5.	Bailliage of Aunis	1337	8	8			
6.	Bailliage of Saintes	672	5	5			
7.	Profits of justice	500	0	0			
	TOTAL RECEIPTS:				3492	19	9

Receipts separated and repeated:

1.	Arrearage from Harduin de Malle	100	0	0			
2.	Debt of the castellan of Saint-Maixent	33	6	8			
	TOTAL:				133	6	8
	REMAINING RECEIPTS:				3359	13	1
	MANUSCRIPT BALANCE:				3363	13	2

Expenses:

1.	Garrison payments	697	10	0			
2.	Clothing for the garrisons	104	7	6			
3.	Miscellaneous expenses	1006	14	4			
4.	Wages of the bailli	93	0	0			
	TOTAL EXPENSES:				1901	11	10
	MANUSCRIPT TOTAL:				1901	10	11

BALANCE DUE TO THE COUNT:		1458	1	3
MANUSCRIPT BALANCE:		2287	9	8

[1]Niort and Saint-Maixent are thus combined in the manuscript. They are again combined in All Saints' Day, 1244.

[2]The "manuscript balance" includes the manuscript "balance due to the count" (which the manuscript erroneously gives as 1462/2/3), arrearages (692/0/9), and extraordinary revenues (133/6/8) for a balance of 2287/9/8.

CANDLEMAS, 1243

SUMMARY ACCOUNT OF THE GENERAL FUND:

REORGANIZED TOTALS

Item	Subtotal			Total		
	l.	s.	d.	l.	s.	d.

Receipts:

1.	Domain receipts						
A.	Domain of the Count of Poitiers	932	3	2			
B.	Domain of Hugh of La Marche	999	19	7			
	TOTAL:				1932	2	9
2.	Arrearage from Harduin de Malle				100	0	0
3.	Debt of the castellan of Saint-Maixent				33	6	8
4.	Payment of Guy le Sénéchal				100	0	0
5.	Relief of the lady of Surgères				50	0	0
6.	Minor reliefs				93	0	0
7.	Redemption of the salt beds of Garnier Nadau				100	0	0
8.	Receipts from Mont-Ravel				57	16	0
9.	Diverse receipts						
A.	Forfeited lands	599	16	1			
B.	Goods of a murderer at Niort	22	16	0			
C.	Castleward of the Lady of Surgères	93	6	8			
D.	Sale of grain and wine at Saintes	23	18	8			
E.	A discovery of iron	11	0	0			
F.	Profits from salt making	19	17	0			
G.	Profits of justice	260	0	0			
	TOTAL:				1030	14	5
	TOTAL RECEIPTS:				3496	19	10

Expenses:

1. Garrison payments
   A. Salaries of the men   697 10 0
   B. Garrison at Saint-Jean-
         d'Angély   23 16 8
   C. Minor expenses   34 9 7
   D. Clothing   104 7 6
         TOTAL: 860 3 9
2. Alms and feudal dues
   A. Feudal dues   457 4 4
   B. Alms   236 1 8
         TOTAL: 693 6 0
3. Public works   145 9 5
4. Minor expenses   110 0 0
5. Wages of the <u>bailli</u>   93 0 0
         TOTAL EXPENSES: 1901 19 2

BALANCE DUE TO THE COUNT: 1595 0 8

CANDLEMAS, 1243

DOMAIN OF THE COUNT OF POITIERS

Item	Revenue		
	l.	s.	d.
1. Provostship of Poitiers	100	0	0
2. Provostship of Niort	106	13	4
3. Provostship of Benon	76	13	4
4. Provostship of La Rochelle	533	6	8
5. Lease revenue at Bourins	16	4	6
6. Pleas at La Rochelle	5	0	0
7. Profits from the forest of Benon	6	10	0
8. Provostship of Saint-Jean-d'Angély	43	6	8
9. Payment by the Jews of Saint-Jean-d'Angély	40	0	0
10. Ripuarian rights at Saint-Anais	1	2	0
11. Ripuarian rights at Saint-Jean-d'Angély	3	6	8
TOTAL	932	3	2

CANDLEMAS, 1243

DOMAIN OF COUNT HUGH DE LA MARCHE

Item	Revenue		
	l.	s.	d.
1. Provostship of Montreuil	103	6	8
2. Sale of wood in the forest of Montreuil	70	0	0
3. Minor customs and revenue from the fair of Sanxay	11	19	7
4. Sale of hay at Sanxay	3	0	0
5. Provostship of Cherveux	33	6	8
6. Sale of cut timber for a house at Cherveux	6	0	0
7. Provostships of Frontenay, Prahecq, and Coulons	146	13	4
8. Provostship of Tonnay-Boutonne	40	0	0
9. Grand fief d'Aunis	383	6	8
10. Sale of extra cut framing timber at Tonnay-Boutonne	10	0	0
11. Rabbits sold at Tonnay-Boutonne	4	10	0
12. Fief of La Croix-Comtesse	26	13	4
13. Provostship of Saintes	128	6	8
14. Lands of Ramegot	11	6	8
15. Lands of Count Hugh de la Marche at Sales	6	13	4
16. Revenues from La Vergne	14	16	8
TOTAL:	999	19	7

33

CANDLEMAS, 1243

GARRISON PAYMENTS

(TERM: 93 Days)

Item	Per Diem			Total		
	l.	s.	d.	l.	s.	d.
1. Poitiers		14	2	65	17	6
2. Sergeant Pozole		7	3	33	14	3
3. Saint-Maixent		16	8	77	10	0
4. Niort	1	17	2	172	16	6
5. Benon		12	11	60	1	3
6. Guy d'Espagne		5	0	23	5	0
7. La Rochelle	2	4	9	208	1	9
8. Surgères		12	1	56	3	9
TOTALS:	7	10	0	697	10	0
MANUSCRIPT TOTAL:				697	10	0

Saint-Jean-d'Angély (65 days)						
(Dec. 6, 1243-Feb. 9, 1244)		7	4	23	16	8
Minor expenses for garrisons				34	9	7
Clothing for the garrisons				104	7	6
FINAL TOTAL:				860	3	9

ASCENSION, 1244

SUMMARY ACCOUNT OF THE GENERAL FUND:

ORIGINAL MANUSCRIPT TOTALS

Item	Subtotal			Total		
	l.	s.	d.	l.	s.	d.

Receipts:

1.	Refund of an overcharge for clothing	3	2	6			
2.	Payment by Jean Aubert	1400	0	0			
3.	Payment by Reginald de Rulle	444	10	6			
4.	Debt of the castellan of Saint-Maixent	16	13	4			
5.	Arrearage from Harduin de Malle	200	4	0			
6.	Bailliage of Poitiers	773	19	4			
7.	Bailliage of Niort	399	17	8			
8.	Bailliage of Aunis	1312	3	4			
9.	Bailliage of Saintes	884	7	7			
10.	Merchant tolls[1]	36	9	6			
11.	Profits of justice	160	0	0			
	TOTAL RECEIPTS:				5631	7	9

Receipts separated and repeated:

1.	Refund of an overcharge for clothing	3	2	6			
2.	Payment by Jean Aubert	1400	0	0			
3.	Payment by Reginald de Rulle	444	10	6			
4.	Debt of the castellan of Saint-Maixent	16	13	4			
5.	Arrearage of Harduin de Malle	200	4	0			
	TOTAL:				2064	10	4
	REMAINING RECEIPTS:				3566	17	5
	MANUSCRIPT BALANCE:				3566	17	5

[1]These "commendisiae" were probably tolls levied on merchants in return for the count's protection while they were passing through his territories. Cf. DuCange, Glossarium mediae et infimae Latinitatis, Vol. II, cols. 850-51 (1733 edition), s.v. "commendisia," and Godefroi, Dictionnaire de l'ancienne langue francaise, Vol. II, p. 192, s.v. "commandise."

Expenses:

1.	Garrison payments	1329	10	0
2.	Alms and feudal dues	239	10	0
3.	Minor expenses	85	6	7
4.	Public works	180	12	6
5.	Wages of the <u>bailli</u>	100	0	0
	TOTAL:	1934	19	1

BALANCE DUE TO THE COUNT:[2]   1631 18 4

[2] The balance due to the count in the manuscript is erroneously stated as 1630/13/4. The manuscript has an overall balance of 4497/12/10 which the accountant arrived at in the following way:

1630	13	4	balance due to the count
802	9	2	arrearage
2064	10	4	extraordinary revenue
4497	12	10	

ASCENSION, 1244

SUMMARY ACCOUNT OF THE GENERAL FUND:

REORGANIZED TOTALS

Item	Subtotal			Total		
	l.	s.	d.	l.	s.	d.
Receipts:						
1. Domain receipts:						
A. Domain of Count Alphonse	1173	3	1			
B. Domain of Hugh de La						
Marche	1417	8	3			
TOTAL DOMAIN RECEIPTS:				2590	11	4
2. Payment of Jean Aubert				1400	0	0
3. Payment of Reginald de Rulle				444	10	6
4. Debt of the castellan of						
Saint-Maixent				16	13	4
5. Arrearage from Harduin de Malle				200	4	0
6. Payment by Guy le Sénéchal				100	0	0
7. Redemption of the salt beds of						
Garnier Nadau				100	0	0
8. Diverse receipts:						
A. Forfeited lands	410	13	9			
B. Relief of the lady of						
Surgères	50	0	0			
C. Castleward at Surgères	46	13	4			
D. Sale of salt at Anatogne	36	3	6			
E. Miscellaneous payments	39	8	6			
F. Merchant tolls	36	9	6			
G. Profits of justice	160	0	0			
TOTAL DIVERSE RECEIPTS:				779	8	7
TOTAL RECEIPTS:				5631	7	9
Expenses:						
1. Garrison payments:						
A. Salaries of the men	1072	14	0			
B. One foot sergeant	1	2	6			
C. Robert de La Vergne	227	11	0			
D. Summer clothing	28	2	6			
TOTAL GARRISON PAYMENTS:				1329	10	0
2. Alms and feudal dues:						
A. Feudal dues	149	3	4			
B. Alms	90	6	8			
TOTAL ALMS AND FEUDAL DUES:				239	10	0

Expenses (continued):

3.	Public works	180	12	6
4.	Minor expenses	86	0	7
5.	Wages of the <u>bailli</u>	100	0	0
	TOTAL EXPENSES:	1935	13	1

BALANCE DUE TO THE COUNT: 3695 14 8

ASCENSION, 1244

DOMAIN OF THE COUNT OF POITIERS

Item	Revenue		
	l.	s.	d.
1. Provostship of Poitiers	100	0	0
2. Sale of wood in the forest of Mouliere	183	6	8
3. Provostship of Niort	106	13	4
4. Minor revenues from Bourins	2	6	5
5. Provostship of La Rochelle	533	6	8
6. Provostship of Benon	76	13	4
7. Sale of wood in the forest of Benon	62	10	0
8. Aids at Boece	60	0	0
9. Lodging rights at Anais	5	0	0
10. Provostship of Saint-Jean-d'Angély	43	6	8
TOTAL:	1173	3	1

ASCENSION, 1244

DOMAIN OF COUNT HUGH DE LA MARCHE

Item	Revenue		
	l.	s.	d.
1. Land of Count Hugh de La Marche at Poitiers	35	0	0
2. Provostship of Montreuil	103	6	8
3. Sale of wood at Montreuil	70	0	0
4. Wood sold to the glassmakers of Montreuil	5	0	0
5. A second sale of wood to the glassmakers	5	0	0
6. Fair and toll revenue at Sanxay	6	12	0
7. Provostships of Frontenay and Prahecq and relief of lodging rights at Saint-Gelais	146	13	4
8. Fief of Cherveux	33	6	8
9. Grand fief of Aunis	383	6	8
10. Provostship of Tonnay-Boutonne	40	0	0
11. Fief of La Croix-Comtesse	26	13	4
12. Provostship of Saintes	128	6	8
13. Minor river dues	7	16	3
14. Fief of Ramegot and Ramiet	11	6	8
15. Sale of wood in the forest of Baconais	395	11	0
16. Minor custons from the forest of Baconais	17	19	0
17. Profits from the forest of Baconais	1	10	0
TOTAL:	1417	8	3

ASCENSION, 1244

GARRISON PAYMENTS

(TERM: 136 DAYS)

Item	Per Diem			Total		
	l.	s.	d.	l.	s.	d.
1. Poitiers		14	2	96	6	8
2. Saint-Maixent		16	8	113	6	8
3. Niort	1	17	2	252	14	8
4. Benon		12	11	87	16	8
5. La Rochelle	2	4	9	304	6	0
6. Saint-Jean-d'Angély		7	9	52	14	0
7. Surgères		12	1	82	3	4
8. Sergeant Pozole		7	3	49	6	0
9. Guy d'Espagne		5	0	34	0	0
TOTALS:	7	17	9	1072	14	0
MANUSCRIPT TOTAL:				1072	14	0
One foot sergeant (27 days)		10		1	2	6
Robert de La Verge in the						
forest of Baconais				227	11	0
Summer clothing				28	2	6
FINAL TOTAL:				1329	10	0
MANUSCRIPT TOTAL:				1329	10	0

ALL SAINTS' DAY, 1244

SUMMARY ACCOUNT OF THE GENERAL FUND:

ORIGINAL MANUSCRIPT TOTALS

Item	Subtotal			Total		
	l.	s.	d.	l.	s.	d.

Receipts:

1.	Payment of Jean Aubert	455	0	0			
2.	Remainder from garrison purchases at Saintes	28	2	6			
3.	Sale of garrison supplies	468	4	1			
4.	Sale of grain	495	11	8			
5.	Payment by Guy le Sénéchal	100	0	0			
6.	Arrearage from Harduin de Malle	100	0	0			
7.	Bailliage of Poitiers	796	13	2			
8.	Bailliage of Niort and Saint-Maixent	696	5	4			
9.	Bailliage of Aunis	1556	3	8			
10.	Bailliage of Saintes	1066	10	9			
11.	Profits of justice	320	0	0			
	TOTAL RECEIPTS:				6082	11	2

Receipts separated and repeated:

1.	Payment by Jean Aubert	455	0	0			
2.	Remainder from garrison purchases at Saintes	28	2	6			
3.	Sale of garrison supplies	468	4	1			
4.	Sale of grain	495	11	8			
5.	Payment by Guy le Sénéchal	100	0	0			
6.	Arrearage from Harduin de Malle	100	0	0			
	TOTAL:				1646	18	3
	REMAINING RECEIPTS:				4435	12	11
	MANUSCRIPT TOTAL:				4435	12	11

Expenses:

1.	Garrison payments	1170	11	9			
2.	Alms and feudal dues	845	10	0			
3.	Garrison supplies and minor expenses	384	2	8			
4.	Public works	94	18	1			
5.	Wages of the bailli	173	0	0			
	TOTAL:				2668	2	6
	MANUSCRIPT TOTAL:				2668	2	6

BALANCE DUE TO THE COUNT:[1]   1767 10   5

---

[1]No balance for the entries of this term is given in the manuscript.

ALL SAINTS' DAY, 1244

SUMMARY ACCOUNT OF THE GENERAL FUND:

REORGANIZED TOTALS

Item	Subtotal			Total		
	l.	s.	d.	l.	s.	d.
Receipts:						
1. Domain receipts:						
A. Domain of Count Alphonse	1162	13	2			
B. Domain of Hugh de La						
Marche	1355	15	0			
TOTAL DOMAIN RECEIPTS:				2518	8	2
2. Payment of Jean Aubert				455	0	0
3. Remainder from garrison						
purchases at Saintes				28	2	6
4. Sale of garrison supplies				468	4	1
5. Sale of grain				495	11	8
6. Payment by Guy le Sénéchal				100	0	0
7. Arrearage from Harduin de Malle				100	0	0
8. Diverse receipts:						
A. Forfeited lands	1145	16	3			
B. Castleward at Surgères	46	13	6			
C. Aids at Champagne	46	10	0			
D. Redemption of the tithe						
at Boece	24	0	0			
E. Sale of the forfeitures in						
the Benonais	334	5	0			
F. Profits of justice	300	0	0			
TOTAL:				1897	4	9
TOTAL RECEIPTS:				6062	11	2
Expenses:						
1. Garrison payments:						
A. Salaries of the men	1142	4	9			
B. Extra garrisons at						
Saintes	28	7	0			
C. Garrison supplies	114	9	2			
TOTAL:				1285	0	11
2. Alms and feudal dues:						
A. Feudal dues	624	3	4			
B. Alms	224	6	8			
TOTAL:				848	10	0
3. Public works				104	18	1
4. Horses bought for the count				160	6	6

Expenses (continued):

5.	Minor expenses	96	7	0
6.	Wages of the <u>bailli</u>	173	0	0
	TOTAL EXPENSES:	2668	2	6

BALANCE DUE TO THE COUNT: 3394 8 8

ALL SAINTS' DAY, 1244

DOMAIN OF THE COUNT OF POITIERS

Item	Revenue		
	l.	s.	d.
1. Provostship of Poitiers	100	0	0
2. Sale in the forest of Moulière	183	6	8
3. Rents of new lands at Moulière	1	15	0
4. Right to enter a new settlement at Moulière	1	10	0
5. Profits from the forest of Moulière	12	0	0
6. Provostship of Niort	106	13	4
7. Lease revenue from Bourins	7	4	10
8. Provostship of La Rochelle	533	6	8
9. Provostship of Benon	76	13	4
10. Lodging rights at Anais	5	0	0
11. Sale of wood in the forest of Benon	62	10	0
12. Payment of the debt of Gautier de Torene	12	0	0
13. Profits from the forest of Benon	14	0	0
14. Provostship of Saint-Jean-d'Angély	43	6	8
15. Minor ripuarian rights at Saint-Jean-d'Angély	3	6	8
TOTAL:	1162	13	2

ALL SAINTS' DAY, 1244

DOMAIN OF COUNT HUGH DE LA MARCHE

Item	Revenue		
	l.	s.	d.
1. Provostship of Montreuil	103	6	8
2. Land of Count Hugh de La Marche at Poitiers	35	0	0
3. Sale of wood in the forest of Montreuil	70	0	0
4. Payment by the glassmakers of Montreuil	5	0	0
5. A second sale of wood to the glassmakers	5	0	0
6. Relief of the Lady of Mondionne	25	0	0
7. Provostship of Frontenay	66	13	4
8. Provostship of Prahecq	60	0	0
9. Provostship of Coulons	6	13	4
10. Provostship of Cherveux	33	6	8
11. Rents and other minor revenues from Sanxay	19	10	4
12. Grand fief of Aunis	383	6	8
13. Provostship of Tonnay-Boutonne	40	0	0
14. Relief of Guiot Serpentin in the Grand fief of Aunis	40	0	0
15. Fief of La Croix-Comtesse	26	13	4
16. Provostship of Saintes	128	6	8
17. Half of a mill on the bridge of Saintes	5	0	0
18. Fief of Ramiet and Ramegot	11	6	8
19. Ripuarian rights at Saint-Anais	2	15	9
20. Fief of the Lady of Contor	5	0	0
21. Arrearage of the Lady of Contor	6	0	0
22. Aids of the abbess of Saintes	175	0	0
23. Aids of Saint-Anais at the feast of St. John	7	0	0
24. Aids of Saint-Anais at the feast of St. Michael	50	0	0
25. Relief of hospitality at Château-Neuf	6	15	4
26. Relief of hospitality at La Vergne	1	3	0
27. Relief of hospitality at Favoux	6	7	9
28. Relief of hospitality at Saint-Gemme	4	7	0
29. Casks of wine sold at La Vergne	13	3	0
30. Hay sold at La Vergne	3	18	0
31. Minor aids and customs	4	11	0
32. Profits from the forest of Baconais	5	10	6
TOTAL:	1355	15	0

ALL SAINTS' DAY, 1244

GARRISON PAYMENTS

(TERM: 137 DAYS)

Item	Per Diem			Total		
	l.	s.	d.	l.	s.	d.
1. Poitiers		14	2	97	0	10
2. Saint-Maixent		16	8	114	3	4
3. Niort	1	17	2	254	11	10
4. Benon		12	11	88	9	7
5. La Rochelle	2	4	9	306	10	9
6. Saint-Jean-d'Angély		7	9	53	1	9
7. Surgère		12	1	82	15	5
8. Sergeant Pozole		7	3	49	13	3
9. Guy d'Espagne		5	0	34	5	0
10. Robert de La Vergne		4	0	27	8	0
11. Adam de Senlis		5	0	34	5	0
TOTAL:	8	6	9	1142	4	9
MANUSCRIPT TOTAL:[1]				1142	4	9
Garrison of the castle of Saintes (7 days)	3	7	3	23	10	9
Garrison of the bridge of Saintes (7 days)		13	9	4	16	3
Supplies for the garrisons				114	9	2
FINAL TOTAL:				1285	0	11

[1] This entry is the sum of the individual items because no total is given in the manuscript.

CANDLEMAS, 1244

SUMMARY ACCOUNT OF THE GENERAL FUND:

ORIGINAL MANUSCRIPT TOTALS

Item	Subtotal			Total		
	l.	s.	d.	l.	s.	d.
Receipts:						
1. Domain of Count Alphonse	1313	9	6			
2. Domain of Hugh de La Marche	1423	9	6			
3. Forfeited lands	575	9	11			
4. Profits of justice	129	0	0			
TOTAL RECEIPTS:				3441	8	11
Expenses:						
1. Garrison payments	1103	11	0			
2. Reinforcements for the garrisons	396	3	5			
3. Traveling expenses	129	7	11			
4. Leave payments	57	6	4			
5. Supplies for the garrisons	364	7	0			
6. Alms and feudal dues	423	0	0			
7. Public works	577	0	1			
8. Minor expenses and wages of the <u>bailli</u>	178	18	4			
TOTAL EXPENSES:				3229	14	1
MANUSCRIPT TOTAL:				3229	14	1
BALANCE DUE TO THE COUNT:				211	14	10
MANUSCRIPT BALANCE:				211	14	10

CANDLEMAS, 1244

SUMMARY ACCOUNT OF THE GENERAL FUND:

REORGANIZED TOTALS

Item	Subtotal			Total		
	l.	s.	d.	l.	s.	d.
Receipts:						
1. Domain receipts:						
A. Domain of Count Alphonse	1313	9	6			
B. Domain of Hugh de La						
Marche	1423	9	6			
TOTAL DOMAIN RECEIPTS:				2736	19	0
2. Diverse receipts:						
A. Forfeited lands	575	10	11			
B. Profits of justice	129	0	0			
TOTAL:				704	10	11
TOTAL RECEIPTS:				3441	9	11
Expenses:						
1. Garrison payments:						
A. Salaries of the men	954	16	0			
B. Leave payments	57	7	6			
C. Clothing, reinforcements						
and supplies	1034	13	1			
TOTAL:				2046	16	7
2. Alms and feudal dues						
A. Feudal dues	349	13	4			
B. Alms	73	6	8			
TOTAL:				423	0	0
3. Public works				577	0	1
4. Minor expenses				85	18	4
5. Wages of the <u>bailli</u>				93	0	0
TOTAL EXPENSES:				3225	15	0
BALANCE DUE TO THE COUNT:				215	14	11

CANDLEMAS, 1244

DOMAIN OF THE COUNT OF POITIERS

Item	Revenue		
	l.	s.	d.
1. Provostship of Poitiers	100	0	0
2. Pasturing pigs in the forest of Mouliere	127	10	0
3. Provostship of Niort	106	13	4
4. Relief of Hugh Jodoin	37	10	0
5. Wardship at Boruns	8	16	2
6. Provostship of Benon	76	13	4
7. Pasturing pigs in the forest of Benon	200	0	0
8. Provostship of La Rochelle	533	6	8
9. Provostship of Saint-Jean-d'Angély	43	6	8
10. Farm of the Jews at Saint-Jean-d'Angély	40	0	0
11. Profits from the forest of Benon	14	13	4
12. Relief of the lady of Mondionne	25	0	0
TOTAL:	1313	9	6
MANUSCRIPT TOTAL:	1313	9	6

DOMAIN OF COUNT HUGH DE LA MARCHE

Item	Revenue		
	l.	s.	d.
1. Provostship of Montreuil	103	6	8
2. Sale in the forest of Montreuil	70	0	0
3. Sale in the woods of Vaumaingot	40	0	0
4. Pasturing pigs in the forest of Montreuil	160	0	0
5. Fief of Cherveux	33	6	8
6. From Sanxay	11	0	0
7. Provostship of Frontenay	66	13	4
8. Provostship of Prahecq	60	0	0
9. Provostship of Coulons	6	13	4
10. Grand fief of Aunis	383	6	8
11. Provostship of Tonnay-Boutonne	40	0	0
12. Fief of La Croix-Comtesse	26	13	4
13. Provostship of Saintes	128	6	8
14. Fief of Ramegot and Ramiet	11	6	8
15. Minor dues and customs around La Vergne	2	18	4
16. Pasturing pigs in the forest of Baconais	142	18	0
17. Profits from the forest of Baconais	1	10	0
18. Minor dues and tolls	11	4	10
19. Fief of the Lady of Contor	5	0	0
20. Sale in the forest of Baconais	119	5	0
TOTAL:	1423	9	6
MANUSCRIPT TOTAL:	1423	9	6

CANDLEMAS, 1244

GARRISON PAYMENTS

(TERM: 93 DAYS)

Item	Per Diem			Total		
	l.	s.	d.	l.	s.	d.
1. Poitiers		14	2	65	17	6
2. Saint-Maixent		16	8	77	10	0
3. Niort	1	14	8	161	4	0
4. Benon		12	11	60	1	3
5. La Rochelle	2	2	9	198	15	9
6. Saintes (castle)	2	1	5	192	11	9
7. Saintes (bridge)		6	8	31	0	0
8. Saint-Jean-d'Angély		7	9	36	0	9
9. Surgères		12	1	56	3	9
10. Sergeant Pozole		7	3	33	14	3
11. Guy d'Espagne		5	0	23	5	0
12. Robert de La Vergne		4	0	18	12	0
TOTAL:	10	5	4	954	16	0
MANUSCRIPT TOTAL:	10	5	4	954	16	0

Winter clothing for the garrisons				148	15	0
Reinforcements for the garrisons				401	3	5
Traveling expenses				120	7	8
Leave payments for garrison troops						
1. Saintes (castle) (30 days)						
(Nov. 8-Dec. 8, 1244)	1	5	10	38	15	0
2. Wages of a knight (8 days)		7	6	3	0	0
3. Saintes (bridge) (30 days)						
(Nov. 8-Dec. 8, 1244)		7	1	10	12	6
4. Pardus (15 days)						
(Nov. 8-Nov. 23, 1244)		2	6	1	17	6
5. Winter clothing for Pardus				3	2	6
TOTAL LEAVE PAYMENTS:				57	7	6
MANUSCRIPT TOTAL:				57	7	6
Supplies for the garrisons				364	7	0
FINAL TOTAL:				2046	16	7

ASCENSION, 1245

SUMMARY ACCOUNT OF THE GENERAL FUND:

ORIGINAL MANUSCRIPT TOTALS

Item	Subtotal			Total		
	l.	s.	d.	l.	s.	d.
Receipts:						
1. Domain of Count Alphonse	1279	4	4			
2. Domain of Hugh de La Marche	1518	6	6			
3. Forfeited lands	485	9	10			
4. Profits of justice	375	10	0			
TOTAL RECEIPTS:				3658	10	8
MANUSCRIPT TOTAL:				3658	10	8
Expenses:						
1. Garrison payments	1405	13	9			
2. Alms and feudal dues	262	0	0			
3. Public works	364	7	9			
4. Minor expenses	173	11	2			
TOTAL EXPENSES:				2205	12	8
MANUSCRIPT TOTAL:				2205	12	8
BALANCE DUE TO THE COUNT:				1452	18	0
MANUSCRIPT BALANCE:				1452	18	0

ASCENSION, 1245

SUMMARY ACCOUNT OF THE GENERAL FUND:

REORGANIZED TOTALS

Item	Subtotal			Total		
	l.	s.	d.	l.	s.	d.
Receipts:						
1. Domain receipts:						
A. Domain of Count Alphonse	1279	4	4			
B. Domain of Hugh de La Marche	1521	6	5			
TOTAL DOMAIN RECEIPTS:				2800	10	9
2. Diverse receipts:						
A. Total forfeitures	485	15	2			
B. Profits of justice	375	10	0			
TOTAL DIVERSE RECEIPTS:				861	5	2
TOTAL RECEIPTS:				3661	15	11
Expenses:						
1. Garrison payments:						
A. Salaries of the men	1371	18	9			
B. Summer clothing	33	15	0			
TOTAL:				1405	13	9
2. Alms and feudal dues						
A. Feudal dues	149	3	4			
B. Alms	112	16	8			
TOTAL:				262	0	0
3. Public works				364	6	9
4. Minor expenses				62	0	8
5. Wages of the bailli				112	0	0
TOTAL EXPENSES:				2206	1	2
BALANCE DUE TO THE COUNT:				1455	14	9

DOMAIN OF THE COUNT OF POITIERS

Item	Revenue		
	l.	s.	d.
1. Provostship of Poitiers	100	0	0
2. The forest of Moulière	183	6	8
3. Relief of the Lady of Mondionne	25	0	0
4. Provostship of Niort	106	13	4
5. Richard le Cuisinier, for the relief of the fief of Bourins	30	0	0
6. Provostship of Benon	66	13	4
7. Sale in the forest of Benon	62	10	0
8. Lodging rights at Anais	5	0	0
9. Provostship of La Rochelle	533	6	8
10. Provostship of Saint-Jean-d'Angély	43	6	8
11. Second sale in the forest of Benon	113	6	8
12. Profits from the forest of Benon	10	1	0
TOTAL:	1279	4	4
MANUSCRIPT TOTAL:	1279	4	4

DOMAIN OF COUNT HUGH DE LA MARCHE

Item	Revenue		
	l.	s.	d.
1. Land of Count Hugh de La Marche at Poitiers	35	0	0
2. Provostship of Montreuil	103	6	8
3. Sale of the forest of Montreuil	70	0	0
4. Forest of Vaumaingot	40	0	0
5. Fief of Cherveux	33	6	8
6. Fief of Fors and sale of Sanxay	8	16	6
7. Provostship of Frontenay	66	13	4
8. Farm of Prahecq	60	0	0
9. Fief of Coulon	6	13	4
10. Grand fief of Aunis	383	6	8
11. Provostship of Tonnay-Boutonne	40	0	0
12. Fief of La Croix-Comtesse	26	13	3
13. Provostship of Saintes	128	6	8
14. Fief of Ramegot and Ramiet	11	6	8
15. Minor revenues from around La Vergne	9	3	0
16. Profits from the forest of Baconais	8	2	0
17. Sale of the forest of Baconais	186	13	4
18. Arrears on the sale of Baconais	275	17	0
19. Minor river dues "in Martugnia"	8	1	4
20. Forest of Saint-Hilaire	5	0	0
21. Plea revenues at Tonnay-Boutonne	5	0	0
22. Fief of the Lady of Contor	5	0	0
23. Dead wood sold to P. Groliau	5	0	0
TOTAL:	1521	6	5
MANUSCRIPT TOTAL:	1518	6	6

ASCENSION, 1245

GARRISON PAYMENTS

(TERM: 135 DAYS)

Item	Per Diem			Total		
	l.	s.	d.	l.	s.	d.
1. Poitiers		12	1	81	11	3
2. Saint-Maixent		16	8	112	10	0
3. Niort	1	14	8	234	0	0
4. Benon		12	11	87	3	9
5. La Rochelle	2	2	9	288	11	3
6. Saint-Jean-d'Angély		7	9	52	6	3
7. Saintes (castle)	2	1	5	279	11	3
8. Saintes (bridge)		6	8	45	0	0
9. Surgères		12	1	81	11	3
10. Sergeant Pozole		7	3	48	18	9
11. Guy d'Espagne		5	0	33	15	0
12. Robert de Gondreville		4	0	27	0	0
TOTALS:	10	3	3	1371	18	9
MANUSCRIPT TOTAL:				1371	18	9
Summer clothing				33	15	0
FINAL TOTAL:				1405	13	9
MANUSCRIPT TOTAL:				1405	13	9

ASCENSION, 1245

SUMMARY ACCOUNT OF THE ROYAL FUND IN POITOU

Item	Subtotal			Total		
	l.	s.	d.	l.	s.	d.
Receipts:						
1. Count of La Marche for castleward				400	0	0
2. Forfeited lands at Angoulême				74	10	0
TOTAL RECEIPTS:				474	10	0
Expenses:						
1. Garrison payments:						
A. Salaries of the men	532	19	0			
B. Garnier de Sule for clothing	6	5	0			
C. The smith at Merpins	1	9	4			
TOTAL:				540	13	4
2. Public works				23	15	0
3. Feudal dues				50	0	0
4. Purchase of food[1]				52	10	5
TOTAL EXPENSES				666	18	9
BALANCE DUE TO THE KING				-192	8	9

[1]This expense is given in _livres de La Marche_ and converted in the manuscript into _livres tournois_. The conversion is: 65 _libr._, 13 _sol._ La Marche multiplied by .8 equals 52 _libr._, 10 _sol._, 5 _den._ Tournois.

ASCENSION, 1245

GARRISON PAYMENTS FOR THE ROYAL ACCOUNT

(TERM: 228 DAYS)[1]

Item	Per Diem			Total		
	l.	s.	d.	l.	s.	d.
1. Merpins	1	8	4	323	0	0
2. Château Achard		15	5	175	15	0
3. Gerbert d'Erbert		3	0	34	4	0
TOTALS:	2	6	9	532	19	0
MANUSCRIPT TOTAL:				512	14	0
Garnier de Sule for summer and winter clothing				6	5	0
The smith at Merpins				1	9	4
FINAL TOTAL:				540	13	4
MANUSCRIPT TOTAL:				540	13	4

[1]This term extended from November 8, 1244 to June 24, 1245.

ACCOUNTS INDEPENDENT OF THE BAILLI

Item	Total
	l. s. d.

1. Bernard de Curie for his military
   service (paid to the count) [1]   100 0 0
2. Profits of justice from the assessors   50 10 0
3. The mintmasters of Saint-Severin   40 0 0

[1]This figure is given by Bardonnet but it is not verifiable in the manuscript because the text is partially effaced.

ALL SAINTS' DAY, 1245

SUMMARY ACCOUNT OF THE GENERAL FUND:

ORIGINAL MANUSCRIPT TOTALS

Item	Subtotal			Total		
	l.	s.	d.	l.	s.	d.
Receipts:						
1. Domain of Count Alphonse	1453	14	3			
2. Domain of Hugh de La Marche	1551	4	5			
3. Forfeited lands	1089	14	9			
4. Fief of Marans and Mauze	504	12	2			
5. Profits of justice	500	0	0			
TOTAL RECEIPTS:				5099	5	7
MANUSCRIPT TOTAL:				5099	5	7
Expenses:						
1. Garrison payments	1392	5	3			
2. Alms and feudal dues	745	10	0			
3. Public works	638	13	2			
4. Minor expenses	105	17	0			
5. Personal expenses of the count	241	7	4			
6. Wages of the <u>bailli</u>	160	0	0			
TOTAL EXPENSES:				3283	12	9
BALANCE DUE TO THE COUNT:				1815	12	10
MANUSCRIPT BALANCE:				1815	12	10

```
                    ALL SAINTS' DAY, 1245

          SUMMARY ACCOUNT OF THE GENERAL FUND:

                    REORGANIZED TOTALS

        Item                    Subtotal        Total

                              l.  s.  d.      l.  s.  d.

Receipts:

1.  Domain receipts:
    A.  Domain of Count Alphonse  1453 14  3
    B.  Domain of Hugh de La
        Marche                    1551  4  5
        TOTAL DOMAIN RECEIPTS:                3004 18  8
2.  Diverse receipts:
    A.  Forfeited lands           1089  9  8
    B.  Fief of Marans and Mauze   499  7  5
    C.  Profits of justice         491  0  0
        TOTAL DIVERSE RECEIPTS:               2079 17  1

        TOTAL RECEIPTS:                       5084 15  9

Expenses:

1.  Garrison payments:
    -salaries of the men          1392  5  3  1392  5  3
2.  Alms and feudal dues:
    A.  Feudal dues                699  3  4
    B.  Alms                        46  6  8
        TOTAL:                                 745 10  0
3.  Public works                                638 13  2
4.  Personal expenses of the count              241  7  4
5.  Minor expenses                              105 17  0
6.  Wages of the bailli                         160  0  0

        TOTAL EXPENSES:                       3283 12  9

BALANCE DUE TO THE COUNT:                     1801  3  0
```

ALL SAINTS' DAY, 1245

DOMAIN OF THE COUNT OF POITIERS

Item	Revenue		
	l.	s.	d.
1. Provostship of Poitiers	100	0	0
2. Sale in the forest of Moulière	183	6	8
3. Relief of the Lady of Mondionne	25	0	0
4. Provostship of Niort	106	13	4
5. Provostship of Benon	76	13	4
6. Sale in the forest of Benon	62	10	0
7. Lodging rights at Anais	5	0	0
8. Aids at Boece	60	0	0
9. Provostship of La Rochelle	533	6	8
10. Provostship of Saint-Jean-d'Angély	43	6	8
11. Second sale in the forest of Benon	113	6	8
12. Increased bid on the first sale in the forest of Benon	18	15	0
13. Rents at Moulière	1	15	0
14. Profits from the forest of Moulière	14	8	0
15. Goods forfeited by a murderer	4	4	9
16. Refief of Guillaume de Lazai	15	0	0
17. The Lady of Crollant	20	0	0
18. Relief of Maingot Raicle	6	0	0
19. Relief of Gascheria[1]	10	0	0
20. Increased bid on the second sale in the forest of Benon	8	6	8
21. Right of inspecting measures (from H. Bernard)	26	1	6
22. Relief of Guy d'Espagne	10	0	0
23. Relief of Guy de Saint-Loup	10	0	0
TOTAL:	1453	14	3
MANUSCRIPT TOTAL:	1453	14	3

[1]This entry was effaced in the manuscript. It is recreated by substracting the other twenty-two items from the manuscript total.

DOMAIN OF COUNT HUGH DE LA MARCHE

Item	Revenue		
	l.	s.	d.
1. Land of Count Hugh de La Marche at Poitiers	35	0	0
2. Provostship of Montreuil	103	6	8
3. Sale in the forest of Montreuil	70	0	0
4. Fief of Cherveux	33	6	8
5. Fief, fair, and sales at Sanxay	15	7	0
6. Provostship of Frontenay	66	13	4
7. Provostship of Prahecq	60	0	0
8. Provostship of Coulon	6	13	4
9. Grand fief of Aunis	383	6	8
10. Provostship of Tonnay-Boutonne	40	0	0
11. Fief of La Croix-Comtesse	26	13	4
12. Provostship of Saintes and fief of Ramegot	133	6	8
13. Sale in the forest of Baconais	186	13	4
14. Relief of hospitality at Château-Neuf	6	4	0
15. Relief of hospitality at La Vergne	1	1	0
16. Relief of hospitality at Favaux	6	7	9
17. Relief of hospitality at Saint-Gemme	4	7	0
18. Aids of the abbot of Saintes at the feast of St. Michael	175	0	0
19. Aids of Saint-Anais at the feast of St. John	7	0	0
20. Aids of Saint-Anais at the feast of St. Michael	50	0	0
21. Fief of the Lady of Contor	5	0	0
22. Arrearages from the sale at Baconais	116	0	0
23. Pleas and rent from P. de Bessia		15	0
24. From Tachet	2	0	0
25. Tithe from Affre	1	0	0
26. Minor river dues and customs from Marennes	8	0	8
27. Profits from the forest of Baconais	5	2	0
28. Vineyard harvests at La Vergne	3	0	0
TOTAL:	1551	4	5
MANUSCRIPT TOTAL:	1551	4	5

ALL SAINTS' DAY, 1245

ACCOUNT OF THE FIEF OF MARANS AND MAUZE

Item	Subtotal			Total		
	l.	s.	d.	l.	s.	d.
Receipts:						
1. Provostship of Marans	140	0	0			
2. Provostship of Mauze	13	6	8			
3. Tolls at Mauze	119	18	0			
4. Other receipts	313	9	4			
TOTAL RECEIPTS:				586	14	0
Expenses:						
1. Total daily payments	78	11	6			
2. Other expenses	8	15	0			
TOTAL EXPENSES:				87	6	6
BALANCE DUE TO THE COUNT:				499	7	6
Additional figures given in the manuscript:						
Receipts				592	4	0
Expenses				87	11	10
Balance due to the count				504	12	2

ALL SAINTS' DAY, 1245

GARRISON PAYMENTS

(TERM: 137 DAYS)

Item	Per Diem			Total		
	l.	s.	d.	l.	s.	d.
1. Poitiers		12	1	82	15	5
2. Saint-Maixent		16	8	114	3	4
3. Niort	1	14	8	237	9	4
4. Benon		12	11	88	9	7
5. La Rochelle	2	2	9	292	16	9
6. Saint-Jean-d'Angély		7	9	53	1	9
7. Saintes (castle)	2	1	5	283	14	1
8. Saintes (bridge)		6	8	45	13	4
9. Surgères		12	1	82	15	5
10. Sergeant Pozole		7	3	49	13	3
11. Guy d'Espagne		5	0	34	5	0
12. Robert de Gondreville		4	0	27	8	0
TOTAL:	10	3	3	1392	5	3
MANUSCRIPT TOTAL:				1392	5	3

ALL SAINTS' DAY, 1245

SUMMARY ACCOUNT OF THE ROYAL FUND IN POITOU

Item	Total
	l. s. d.
Receipts:	
County of La Marche for castleward	133 6 8
Expenses:	
Garrison payments (salaries of the men)	320 4 9
BALANCE DUE TO THE KING:	-186 18 1

SUMMARY ACCOUNT OF THE GENERAL FUND:

ORIGINAL MANUSCRIPT TOTALS

Item	Subtotal			Total		
	l.	s.	d.	l.	s.	d.
Receipts:						
1. Domain of Count Alphonse	1050	10	0			
2. Domain of Hugh de La Marche	1297	7	7			
3. Forfeited lands	669	14	7			
4. Fief of Marans and Mauze	399	14	6			
5. Grand fief of Aunis	1000	0	0			
6. Profits of justice	282	10	0			
TOTAL RECEIPTS:				4699	16	8
MANUSCRIPT TOTAL:				4699	16	10
Expenses:						
1. Garrison payments	1071	6	2			
2. Alms and feudal dues	473	0	0			
3. Public works	155	11	1			
4. Minor expenses	64	9	5			
5. Expenses of Marans and Mauze	98	6	6			
6. Wages of the <u>bailli</u>	93	0	0			
TOTAL EXPENSES:				1955	13	2
MANUSCRIPT TOTAL:				1955	13	2
BALANCE DUE TO THE COUNT:				2744	3	6
MANUSCRIPT BALANCE:				2744	3	8

CANDLEMAS, 1245

SUMMARY ACCOUNT OF THE GENERAL FUND:

REORGANIZED TOTALS

Item	Subtotal			Total		
	l.	s.	d.	l.	s.	d.
Receipts:						
1. Domain receipts:						
A. Domain of Count Alphonse	1050	10	0			
B. Domain of Hugh de La Marche	1297	10	7			
TOTAL DOMAIN RECEIPTS:				2348	0	7
2. Diverse receipts:						
A. Forfeited lands	669	14	7			
B. Fief of Marans and Mauze	304	6	0			
C. Profits of justice	282	10	0			
D. Grand fief of Aunis	1000	0	0			
TOTAL DIVERSE RECEIPTS:				2256	10	7
TOTAL RECEIPTS:				4604	11	2
Expenses:						
1. Garrison payments:						
A. Salaries of the men	915	5	6			
B. Wages of two sergeants who died during the term	14	3	4			
C. Expenses for clothing	141	17	4			
TOTAL:				1071	6	2
2. Alms and feudal dues:						
A. Feudal dues	149	13	4			
B. Alms	323	6	8			
TOTAL				473	0	0
3. Public works				165	11	1
4. Minor expenses				64	9	11
5. Wages of the bailli				93	0	0
TOTAL EXPENSES:				1867	7	2
BALANCE DUE TO THE COUNT:				2737	4	0

CANDLEMAS, 1245

DOMAIN OF THE COUNT OF POITIERS

Item	Revenue		
	l.	s.	d.
1. Provostship of Poitiers	100	0	0
2. Provostship of Niort	106	13	4
3. Provostship of Benon	76	13	4
4. Provostship of La Rochelle	533	6	8
5. Provostship of Saint-Jean-d'Angély	43	6	8
6. Farm of the Jews at Saint-Jean-d'Angély	40	0	0
7. Profits from the forest of Benon	6	0	0
8. Second sale in the forest of Benon	113	6	8
9. Increased bid on this sale at Benon	4	3	4
10. Right of inspecting measures at La Rochelle	15	0	0
11. Pleas from the fief of the deceased P. de Roche	6	0	0
12. Wine customs at Niort	6	0	0
TOTAL:	1050	10	0
MANUSCRIPT TOTAL:	1050	10	0

CANDLEMAS, 1245

DOMAIN OF COUNT HUGH DE LA MARCHE

Item	Revenue		
	l.	s.	d.
1. Provostship of Montreuil	103	6	8
2. Fief of Cherveux	33	6	8
3. Forfeited lands at Sanxay	7	16	5
4. Provostship of Frontenay	76	13	4
5. Provostship of Prahecq	60	0	0
6. Provostship of Coulons	6	13	4
7. Grand fief of Aunis	416	16	4
8. Provostship of Tonnay-Boutonne	40	0	0
9. Fief of La Croix-Comtesse	26	13	4
10. Provostship of Saintes and fief of Ramegot	133	6	8
11. Pasturage rights in the forest of Baconais	2	2	0
12. Minor customs near the forest of Baconais	6	7	0
13. Minor customs and water rights	2	19	6
14. Profits from the forest of Baconais	2	15	0
15. Sale in the forest of Montreuil	70	0	0
16. Sale in the forest of Baconais	186	13	4
17. Fief of the Lady of Contor	5	0	0
18. Relief of Guillaume de Sirre	12	0	0
19. Fief of Tonnay-Boutone and other lands	46	14	4
20. Sale in the woods of Vaumaingot	40	0	0
21. Sale in the woods of Vitre	5	0	0
22. Sale of rabbits at Tonnay-Boutonne	13	6	8
TOTAL:	1297	10	7
MANUSCRIPT TOTAL:	1297	10	7

CANDLEMAS, 1245

GARRISON PAYMENTS

(TERM: 93 DAYS)

Item	Per Diem			Total		
	l.	s.	d.	l.	s.	d.
1. Poitiers		12	1	56	3	9
2. Saint-Maixent		16	8	77	10	0
3. Niort	1	12	10	152	13	6
4. Benon		12	11	60	1	3
5. La Rochelle	2	2	9	198	15	9
6. Saint-Jean-d'Angély		7	9	36	0	9
7. Saintes (castel)	2	1	5	192	11	9
8. Saintes (bridge)		2	1	9	13	9
9. Sergeant Pozole		7	3	33	14	3
10. Guy d'Espagne		5	0	23	5	0
11. Robert de Gondreville		4	0	18	12	0
TOTAL:	9	4	9	859	1	9
MANUSCRIPT TOTAL:				915	5	6
12. Surgeres		12	1	56	3	9
CORRECTED TOTAL:	9	16	10	915	5	6
MANUSCRIPT TOTAL:				915	5	6

Wages for two sergeants who died during the term:

1. Master Laurent (29 days)						
(Nov. 8-Dec. 7, 1245)		2	6	3	12	6
2. Raoul of Anot (46 days)						
(Nov. 8-Dec. 24, 1245)		4	7	10	10	10
TOTAL:				14	3	4
Expenses for clothing				141	17	4
FINAL TOTAL:				1071	6	2
MANUSCRIPT TOTAL:				1071	6	2

CANDLEMAS, 1245

SUMMARY ACCOUNT OF THE ROYAL FUND IN POITOU

Item	Subtotal			Total		
	l.	s.	d.	l.	s.	d.

Receipts:

1.	Forfeited lands at Angoulême				14	0	0
2.	Count of La Marche for castleward				133	6	8
3.	Sale of foodstuffs				111	8	0
	TOTAL:				258	14	8

Expenses:

Garrison payments							
A. Salaries of the men	217	7	9				
B. Expenses for clothing	3	2	6				
TOTAL:					220	10	3

BALANCE DUE TO THE KING: 38 4 5

SUMMARY ACCOUNT OF THE GENERAL FUND:

ORIGINAL MANUSCRIPT TOTALS

Item	Subtotal			Total		
	l.	s.	d.	l.	s.	d.

Receipts:

1.	Domain of Count Alphonse	2515	10	7			
2.	Domain of Hugh de La Marche	1249	9	4			
3.	Forfeited lands	403	19	0			
4.	Redemptions of forfeited lands	509	3	4			
5.	Profits of justice	135	10	0			
	TOTAL RECEIPTS:				4813	12	3
	MANUSCRIPT TOTAL:				4813	12	3

Expenses:

1.	Garrison payments	1400	12	2			
2.	Alms and feudal dues	249	10	0			
3.	Public works	330	6	5			
4.	Minor expenses	227	15	2			
5.	Wages of the bailli	104	0	0			
	TOTAL EXPENSES:				2312	3	9
	MANUSCRIPT TOTAL:				2312	3	9

BALANCE DUE TO THE COUNT: 2501   8   6

MANUSCRIPT BALANCE: 2501   8   6

ASCENSION, 1246

SUMMARY ACCOUNT OF THE GENERAL FUND:

REORGANIZED TOTALS

Item	Subtotal			Total		
	l.	s.	d.	l.	s.	d.
Receipts:						
1. Domain receipts:						
A. Domain of Count Alphonse[1]	2515	10	7			
B. Domain of Hugh de La Marche	1249	9	4			
TOTAL DOMAIN RECEIPTS:				3764	19	11
2. Diverse receipts:						
A. Forfeited lands	403	19	0			
B. Redemptions of forfeited lands	509	3	4			
C. Profits of justice	135	10	0			
TOTAL DIVERSE RECEIPTS:				1048	12	4
TOTAL RECEIPTS:				4813	12	3
Expenses:						
1. Garrison payments:						
A. Salaries of the men	1269	11	3			
B. Payment at Fontenay	68	8	0			
C. Wages of two sergeants who died during the term	24	10	5			
D. Expenses for clothing	38	2	6			
TOTAL:				1400	12	2
2. Alms and feudal dues:						
A. Feudal dues	149	3	4			
B. Alms	100	6	8			
TOTAL:				249	10	0
3. Public works				330	6	5
4. Minor expenses				225	6	2
5. Wages of the bailli				104	0	0
TOTAL EXPENSES:				2309	14	9
BALANCE DUE TO THE COUNT:				2503	7	6

[1]This figure includes a relief of 1000 libr. paid by
Raoul Mauleon.

ASCENSION, 1246

DOMAIN OF THE COUNT OF POITIERS

Item	Revenue		
	l.	s.	d.
1. Provostship of Poïtiers	100	0	0
2. Provostship of Niort	106	13	4
3. Provostship of Benon	76	13	4
4. Provostship of La Rochelle	533	6	8
5. Provostship of Saint-Jean-d'Angély	43	6	8
6. Relief of Raoul of Mauleon	1000	0	0
7. Provostship of Frontenay	133	6	8
8. Sale of 23 arpents of forest land in the forest of Moulière	76	13	4
9. Sale of 323 arpents in the forest of Moulière	159	18	11
10. Sale of 124 arpents in the forest of Moulière	56	16	8
11. Sale in the forest of Benon	113	6	8
12. Lodging rights at Anais	5	0	0
13. Sale in the forest of Benon	62	10	0
14. Increase on the first sale at Benon	4	3	4
15. Increase on the second sale at Benon	18	15	0
16. Profits from the land of Guillaume de Mauze	25	0	0
TOTAL:	2515	10	7
MANUSCRIPT TOTAL:	2515	10	7

DOMAIN OF COUNT HUGH DE LA MARCHE

Item	Revenue l.	s.	d.
1. Land of Count Hugh de La Marche at Poitiers	35	0	0
2. Provostship of Montreuil	103	6	8
3. Fief of Cherveux	33	6	8
4. Fief, fair, and minor customs at Sanxay	5	10	0
5. Provostship of Frontenay	66	13	4
6. Provostship of Prahecq	60	0	0
7. Provostship of Coulons	6	13	4
8. Grand fief of Aunis	416	13	4
9. Provostship of Tonnay-Boutonne	40	0	0
10. Fief of La Croix-Comtesse	26	13	4
11. Provostship of Saintes and the fief of Ramegot	133	6	8
12. Fief of the Lady of Contor	5	0	0
13. Customs on new lands around La Vergne	6	18	0
14. Profits from the forest of Baconais	5	4	0
15. Minor water rights at Marennes		15	8
16. Eels sold at Montreuil	2	15	0
17. Sale in the forest of Baconais	186	13	4
18. Sale in the woods of Vaumaingot	40	0	0
19. Dead wood sold in the forest of Montreuil	5	0	0
20. Sale in the forest of Montreuil	70	0	0
TOTAL:	1249	9	4
MANUSCRIPT TOTAL:	1249	9	4

ASCENSION, 1246

GARRISON PAYMENTS

(TERM: 135 DAYS)

Item	Per Diem			Total		
	l.	s.	d.	l.	s.	d.
1. Poitiers		12	1	81	11	3
2. Saint-Maixent		16	8	112	10	0
3. Niort	1	8	8	193	10	0
4. Benon		12	11	87	3	9
5. Surgères		12	1	81	11	3
6. La Rochelle	1	19	0	263	5	0
7. Saint-Jean-d'Angély		7	9	52	6	3
8. Saintes (castle)	2	0	7	273	18	9
9. Saintes (bridge)		2	1	14	1	3
10. Sergeant Pozole		7	3	48	18	9
11. Guy d'Espagne		5	0	33	15	0
12. Robert de Gondreville		4	0	27	0	0
TOTAL:	9	8	1	1269	11	3
MANUSCRIPT:				1269	11	3

	Per Diem			Total		
Garrison at Fontenay (228 days)						
(Nov. 8-June 24, 1246)		6	0	68	8	0
Wages for two sergeants who died						
during the term:						
1. Robert Damens (56 days)						
(Feb. 9-April 6, 1246)		3	4	9	6	8
2. Alexandre (81 days)		3	9	15	3	9
TOTAL:				24	10	5
Expenses for clothing				38	2	6
FINAL TOTAL:				1400	12	2
MANUSCRIPT TOTAL:				1400	12	2

ASCENSION, 1246

SUMMARY ACCOUNT OF THE ROYAL FUND IN POITOU

Item	Subtotal	Total
	l. s. d.	l. s. d.

Receipts:

  County of La Marche for castleward   133 6 8

Expenses:

  Garrison payments:
1. Salaries of the men	315 11 3	
2. Expenses for clothing	3 2 6	
TOTAL:		318 13 9

BALANCE DUE TO THE KING: -185 7 1

```
                  ALL SAINTS' DAY, 1246

          SUMMARY ACCOUNT OF THE GENERAL FUND:

               ORIGINAL MANUSCRIPT TOTALS

          Item                    Subtotal          Total

                                  l.  s.  d.       l.  s.  d.

Receipts:

1.  Redemptions of forfeited
       lands                      668 13   4
2.  Relief                       1900  0   0
3.  Domain of Count Alphonse     1190  9   4
4.  Domain of Hugh de La
       Marche                    1670  4   6
5.  Forfeited lands               614  6  11
6.  Sale of grain                 274  8   0
7.  Profits of justice            160  0   0
8.  Castleward at Surgères         30  9   2
       TOTAL RECEIPTS:                           6508 11   3

Receipts separated and repeated:

1.  Redemptions of forfeited
       lands                      668 13   4
2.  Reliefs                      1900  0   0
       TOTAL:                                    2568 13   4
       REMAINING RECEIPTS:                       3939 17  11
       MANUSCRIPT BALANCE:                       3939 17  11

Expenses:

1.  Garrison payments            1298 11   2
2.  Alms and feudal dues          754 13   0
3.  Public works                  594 11  10
4.  Minor expenses                100 14   7
5.  Wages of the bailli           168  0   0
       TOTAL EXPENSES:                           2916 10   7
       MANUSCRIPT TOTAL:                         2916 10   7

BALANCE DUE TO THE COUNT:                        1023  7   4
MANUSCRIPT BALANCE:                              1023  7   4
```

ALL SAINTS' DAY, 1246

SUMMARY ACCOUNT OF THE GENERAL FUND:

REORGANIZED TOTALS

Item	Subtotal			Total		
	l.	s.	d.	l.	s.	d.

Receipts:

1.	Domain receipts:						
	A. Domain of Count Alphonse	1190	9	4			
	B. Domain of Hugh de La						
	Marche	1670	6	6			
	TOTAL DOMAIN RECEIPTS:				2860	15	10
2.	Redemptions of forfeited lands				678	13	4
3.	Reliefs				1900	0	0
4.	Diverse receipts:						
	A. Forfeited lands	611	10	10			
	B. Sale of grain	274	8	0			
	C. Castleward at Surgères	30	9	2			
	D. Profits of justice	160	0	0			
	TOTAL DIVERSE RECEIPTS:				1076	8	0
	TOTAL RECEIPTS:				6515	17	2

Expenses:

1.	Garrison payments:						
	A. Salaries of the men	1248	8	3			
	B. Payments at Surgères	50	2	11			
	TOTAL:				1298	11	2
2.	Alms and feudal dues:						
	A. Feudal dues	681	13	4			
	B. Alms	47	19	8			
	TOTAL:				729	13	0
3.	Public works				591	11	10
4.	Minor expenses				100	14	7
5.	Wages of the _bailli_				168	0	0
	TOTAL EXPENSES:				2888	10	7

BALANCE DUE TO THE COUNT: 3627 6 7

ALL SAINTS' DAY, 1246

DOMAIN OF THE COUNT OF POITIERS

Item	Revenue		
	l.	s.	d.
1. Provostship of Poitiers	100	0	0
2. Provostship of Niort	113	6	8
3. Provostship of Benon	80	0	0
4. Provostship of La Rochelle	533	6	8
5. Provostship of Saint-Jean-d'Angély	43	6	8
6. Provostship of Frontenay	66	13	4
7. Lodging rights at Anais	5	0	0
8. Aids at Boece	60	0	0
9. Rents at Moulière	1	16	0
10. A new inn at Moulière	1	0	0
11. Profits from the forest of Moulière	14	0	0
12. Relief of Jean Clareul	30	0	0
13. Sale in the forest of Benon	113	6	8
14. Increased bid on this sale in Benon	4	3	4
15. A hedge sold at Saint-Jean-d'Angély	3	10	0
16. Relief paid by Aimeri de Marreillac	21	0	0
TOTAL:	1190	9	4
MANUSCRIPT TOTAL:	1190	9	4

DOMAIN OF COUNT HUGH DE LA MARCHE

Item	Revenue		
	l.	s.	d.
1. Land of Count Hugh at Poitiers	35	0	0
2. Provostship of Montreuil	126	13	4
3. Fief of Cherveux	33	6	8
4. Fief of Sanxay	13	6	8
5. Provostship of Frontenay	78	6	8
6. Provostship of Coulons	13	6	8
7. Provostshipof Prahecq	73	6	8
8. Grand fief of Aunis	416	13	4
9. Provostship of Tonnay-Boutonne	50	0	0
10. Fief of Graves	7	10	0
11. Fief of La Croix-Comtesse	26	13	4
12. Provostship of Saintes and fief of Ramegot	133	6	8
13. Fief of the Lady of Contor	12	0	0
14. A mill at La Vergne	2	0	0
15. Wine sold from the vineyards of La Vergne	1	4	0
16. Minor rents from La Vergne	1	4	6
17. Grain sold at La Vergne	1	14	0
18. Hay sold at La Vergne	4	10	0
19. Customary revenues in kind		4	0
20. Pasturage rights in the forest of Baconais	2	1	8
21. Profits from the forest of Baconais	10	0	0
22. Minor water rights at Marennes	6	10	8
23. Profits from salt	3	0	0
24. Farm of minor customs from Saint-Gemme, Favaux, and Château-Neuf	20	0	0
25. Aids of the abbess of Saintes	175	0	0
26. Aids from the fief of the prior of Saint-Anais	57	0	0
27. Sale in the forest of Montreuil	71	18	10
28. Sale of wood from Vaumaingot	24	8	10
29. Dead wood sold to the glass makers	7	6	8
30. Sale of wood in the forest of Baconais	186	13	4
31. Arrearages from the sale made by Adam de Senlis in the forest of Baconais	56	0	0
32. Sale in the woods of Tonnay-Boutonne	20	0	0
TOTAL:	1670	6	6
MANUSCRIPT TOTAL:	1670	4	6

[1]The manuscript reading of "XXIII l. VIII s. X d." for this entry has been corrected to conform to the amount given in subsequent terms. The total for this term confirms that amount.

ALL SAINTS' DAY, 1246

GARRISON PAYMENTS

(TERM: 137 DAYS)

Item	Per Diem			Total		
	l.	s.	d.	l.	s.	d.
1. Poitiers		12	1	82	15	5
2. Saint-Maixent		16	8	114	3	4
3. Niort	1	9	11	204	18	7
4. Benon		12	11	88	9	7
5. Saint-Jean-d'Angély		7	9	53	1	9
6. Saintes (castle)	2	0	7	277	19	11
7. Saintes (bridge)		2	1	14	5	5
8. Fontenay		6	0	41	2	0
9. Sergeant Pozole		7	3	49	13	3
10. Robert de Gondreville		4	0	27	8	0
11. Robert le Norman		4	0	27	8	0
TOTALS:	7	3	3	981	5	3
MANUSCRIPT TOTAL:				1248	8	3
12. La Rochelle	1	19	0	267	3	0
CORRECTED TOTALS:	9	2	3	1248	8	3
MANUSCRIPT TOTAL:				1248	8	3

Garrison at Surgeres (83 days)
(June 24-Sept. 15, 1246)

	Per Diem			Total		
(June 24-Sept. 15, 1246)		12	1	50	2	11
FINAL TOTAL:				1298	11	2
MANUSCRIPT TOTAL:				1298	11	2

```
                   ALL SAINTS' DAY, 1246

     SUMMARY ACCOUNT OF THE ROYAL FUND IN POITOU

           Item            Subtotal        Total

                           l.  s.  d.     l.  s.  d.

Receipts:

1.  Sale of foodstuffs:
    A. Chateau Achard       38  7  0
    B. Merpins              58  3  2
       TOTAL:                             96  10  2
2.  County of La Marche for
       castleward                         66  13  4
       TOTAL RECEIPTS:                   163   3  6

Expenses:

1.  Garrison payments                     12  17  6
2.  Two master mariners                    5   0  0
3.  Expenses of the chatelain
       of Merpins                         23   6  3
       TOTAL EXPENSES:                    41   3  9

BALANCE DUE TO THE KING:                 121  19  9
```

CANDLEMAS, 1246

SUMMARY ACCOUNT OF THE GENERAL FUND:

ORIGINAL MANUSCRIPT TOTALS

Item	Subtotal			Total		
	l.	s.	d.	l.	s.	d.

Receipts:

1.	Extraordinary payments to the count	928	3	4			
2.	Reliefs	2200	0	0			
3.	Redemptions of forfeited lands	720	13	11			
4.	Domain of Count Alphonse	1494	14	11			
5.	Domain of Hugh de La Marche	1437	14	6			
6.	Forfeited lands	666	18	0			
7.	Revenues from La Roche-sur-Yon	163	1	6			
8.	Castleward at Tiffauges	40	0	0			
9.	Castleward at Civray	40	0	0			
10.	Profits of justice	310	14	9			
	TOTAL RECEIPTS:				8002	0	4

Receipts separated and repeated:

1.	Extraordinary payments to the count[1]	928	3	4			
2.	Reliefs	2200	0	0			
3.	Redemptions of forfeited lands	720	13	4			
	TOTAL:				3848	16	8
	REMAINING RECEIPTS:				4153	3	8
	MANUSCRIPT TOTAL:				4153	3	8

Expenses:

1.	Garrison payments	1006	5	4			
2.	Garrisons of forfeited lands	266	7	7			
3.	Alms and feudal dues	478	0	0			
4.	Public works	256	10	10			
5.	Minor expenses	94	7	6			
6.	Wages of the bailli	93	0	0			
	TOTAL EXPENSES:				2194	11	3

Expenses (continued):

MANUSCRIPT TOTAL:	2194	11	3
BALANCE DUE TO THE COUNT:	1958	12	5
MANUSCRIPT BALANCE:	1958	12	5

[1]Among the extraordinary sources of income is 552/7/9 received from the mintmasters of La Rochelle for the minting of 11,047/15/0. This represents a 5% royalty to the count.

CANDLEMAS, 1246

SUMMARY ACCOUNT OF THE GENERAL FUND:

REORGANIZED TOTALS

Item	Subtotal			Total		
	l.	s.	d.	l.	s.	d.
Receipts:						
1. Domain receipts						
A. Domain of Count Alphonse	1494	14	11			
B. Domain of Hugh de La Marche	1435	14	6			
TOTAL DOMAIN RECEIPTS:				2930	9	5
2. Reliefs				2200	0	0
3. Redemptions of forfeited lands				718	13	4
4. Extraordinary payments to the count				928	3	4
5. Diverse receipts:						
A. Forfeited lands	666	18	0			
B. Revenues from La Roche-sur-Yon	163	1	6			
C. Castleward at Tiffauges	40	0	0			
D. Castleward at Civray	40	0	0			
E. Profits of justice	288	14	9			
TOTAL DIVERSE RECEIPTS:				1198	14	3
TOTAL RECEIPTS:				7976	0	4
Expenses:						
1. Garrison payments:						
A. Salaries of the men	851	14	6			
B. Winter clothing	131	17	6			
C. Two sergeants at Saintes	22	13	4			
TOTAL:				1006	5	4
2. Garrisons of forfeited lands:						
A. La Roche-sur-Yon	92	0	4			
B. Tiffauges	51	1	5			
C. Civray	26	0	0			
D. Provisions for these garrisons	96	15	0			
TOTAL:				265	16	9
3. Alms and feudal dues:						
A. Feudal dues	400	13	4			
B. Alms	77	6	8			
TOTAL:				478	0	0

Expenses (continued):

4.	Public works	256	10	10
5.	Minor expenses	94	7	6
6.	Wages of the <u>bailli</u>	93	0	0
	TOTAL EXPENSES:	2194	0	5

BALANCE DUE TO THE COUNT: 5781 19 11

CANDLEMAS, 1246

DOMAIN OF THE COUNT OF POITIERS

Item	Revenue		
	l.	s.	d.
1. Provostship of Poitiers	100	0	0
2. Provostship of Niort	113	6	8
3. Provostship of Benon	80	0	0
4. Provostship of La Rochelle	533	6	8
5. Provostship of Saint-Jean-d'Angély	43	6	8
6. Provostship of Fontenay-le-Comte	66	13	4
7. Right of pasturage in the forest of Moulière	5	3	6
8. Right of pasturage in the forest of Benon	50	0	0
9. Profits from the forest of Benon	28	0	0
10. Relief from the fief of Jean Clareuil	30	0	0
11. Pierre de Soonay for the fief of Affre	26	13	4
12. Pierre Bertin for the fief of G. d'Allemagne	33	6	8
13. Sale in the forest of Benon	113	6	8
14. Increased bid on this sale	4	3	4
15. Hilaire Foucher for taking over the old sale of wood from the forest of Moulière	15	0	0
16. Sale of 323 arpents in Moulière	147	15	10
17. Sale of 124 arpents in the same forest	56	16	8
18. Hamenon de la Roche for his wife's relief	40	0	0
19. Profits from the fief of Ardannes	5	15	7
20. Relief from the fief of Barraud	2	0	0
TOTAL:	1494	14	11
MANUSCRIPT TOTAL:	1494	14	11

DOMAIN OF COUNT HUGH DE LA MARCHE

Item	Revenue		
	l.	s.	d.
1. Provostship of Montreuil	126	13	4
2. Farm of Cherveux	33	6	8
3. Fief of Sanxay	13	6	8
4. Provostship of Frontenay	78	6	8
5. Increased bid on Frontenay (two terms)	10	0	0
6. Farm of Coulons	13	6	8
7. Farm of Prahecq	73	6	8
8. Frand fief of Aunis	416	13	4
9. Provostship of Tonnay-Boutonne	50	0	0
10. Fief of La Croix-Comtesse	26	13	4
11. Provostship of Saintes and fief of Romegot and Ramiet	133	6	8
12. Pasturage rights in the forest of Baconais	40	0	0
13. Entry into office of theforester in Baconais	20	0	0
14. Profits from the forest of Baconais	4	0	0
15. Customary dues from around La Vergne		11	6
16. Dues from Favaux and Château-Neuf	20	0	0
17. Ripuarian rights at Saint-Jean-d'Angély	2	6	8
18. Minor ripuarian rights	2	2	0
19. Sale in the forest of Montreuil	71	18	10
20. Sale in the forest of Vaumaingot	24	8	10
21. Dead wood sold to the glassmakers in Vaumaingot	7	6	8
22. Sale in the forest of Baconais	186	13	4
23. From the forest and warren of Tonnay-Boutonne	20	0	0
24. Rabbits sold at Tonnay-Boutonne	8	0	0
25. Hugh de Burli for the relief of the fief of Geoffroi Lestor	20	0	0
26. Rabbits sold from the warren of Frontenay	9	6	8
27. Relief of the fief of Aymeri de Mont-Buell	10	0	0
28. Two shares of the mills on the bridge of Saintes	14	0	0
TOTAL:	1435	14	6
MANUSCRIPT TOTAL:	1437	14	6

CANDLEMAS, 1246

GARRISON PAYMENTS

(TERM: 93 DAYS)

Item	Per Diem			Total		
	l.	s.	d.	l.	s.	d.
1. Poitiers		12	1	56	3	9
2. Saint-Maixent		16	8	77	10	0
3. Niort	1	9	2	135	12	6
4. Benon		12	11	60	1	3
5. La Rochelle	1	19	0	181	7	0
6. Saint-Jean-d'Angély		7	9	36	0	9
7. Saintes (castle)	2	2	3	196	9	3
8. Saintes (bridge)		2	1	9	13	9
9. Fontenay-le-Comte		6	0	27	18	0
10. Sergeant Pozole		7	3	33	14	3
11. Robert de Gondreville		4	0	18	12	0
12. Robert le Norman		4	0	18	12	0
TOTAL:	9	3	2	851	14	6

Clothing for the garrisons				131	17	6
Two sergeants at Saintes (272 days) (Feb. 9-Nov. 8, 1246)		1	8	22	13	4
FINAL TOTAL:				1006	5	4
MANUSCRIPT TOTAL:				1006	5	4

CANDLEMAS, 1246

GARRISON PAYMENTS IN FORFEITED LANDS

Item	Per Diem			Total		
	l.	s.	d.	l.	s.	d.

La Roche-sur-Yon:

1.	Pierre de Vicinis (for 3 archers and 6 sergeants)	(no daily rate)				17	5	8
2.	Martin Alphonse (80 days) (Oct. 25, 1245-Jan. 13, 1246)		6	8		26	13	4
3.	Martin Alphonse (for sergeants and archers)	(no daily rate)				39	1	4
4.	Garrison of the castle at La Roche-sur-Yon (27 days) (Jan. 13-Feb. 9, 1246)		6	8		9	0	0
	TOTAL:					92	0	4

Tiffauges:

1.	Garrison of the castle at Tiffauges	(no daily rate)				16	12	5
2.	Thibaut de Campagne (39 days) (Jan. 1-Feb. 9, 1246)		17	8		34	9	0
	TOTAL:					51	1	5

Civray:

Garrison of the castle at Civray	(no daily rate)	26	0	0
TOTAL GARRISONS:		169	1	9
MANUSCRIPT TOTAL:		169	12	7
Provisions for these garrisons		96	15	0
TOTAL PAYMENTS:		265	16	9
MANUSCRIPT TOTAL:		266	7	7

SUMMARY ACCOUNT OF THE GENERAL FUND:

ORIGINAL MANUSCRIPT TOTALS

Item	Subtotal			Total		
	l.	s.	d.	l.	s.	d.
Receipts:						
1. Reliefs	2050	0	0			
2. Redemptions of forfeited lands	593	16	8			
3. Assessment of the Jews	500	0	0			
4. Domain of Count Alphonse	1253	5	10			
5. Domain of Hugh de La Marche	1255	13	0			
6. Forfeited lands	418	1	6			
7. Revenues from La Roche-sur-Yon	73	13	6			
8. Castleward at Tiffauges	40	0	0			
9. Castleward at Civray	40	0	0			
10. Sale of wheat and other grains	250	1	6			
11. Profits of justice	212	17	6			
TOTAL RECEIPTS:				6687	9	6
Receipts separated and repeated:						
1. Reliefs	2050	0	0			
2. Redemptions of forfeited lands	593	16	8			
3. Assessment of the Jews	500	0	0			
TOTAL:				3143	16	8
REMAINING RECEIPTS:				3543	12	10
MANUSCRIPT TOTAL:				3543	12	10

Expenses:

1.	Garrison payments	1507	6	8
2.	Alms and feudal dues	247	0	0
3.	Public works	129	10	0
4.	Minor expenses	106	19	9
5.	Wages of the <u>bailli</u>	96	0	0

TOTAL EXPENSES:	2086	16	5
MANUSCRIPT TOTAL:	2086	16	5
BALANCE DUE TO THE COUNT:	1456	16	5
MANUSCRIPT BALANCE:	1456	16	5

ASCENSION, 1247

SUMMARY ACCOUNT OF THE GENERAL FUND:

REORGANIZED TOTALS

Item	Subtotal			Total		
	l.	s.	d.	l.	s.	d.

Receipts:

1. Domain receipts:						
A. Domain of Count Alphonse	1253	5	10			
B. Domain of Hugh de La Marche	1255	13	0			
TOTAL DOMAIN RECEIPTS:				2508	18	10
2. Reliefs				2050	0	0
3. Redemptions of forfeited lands				593	16	8
4. Redemption of the goods of the Jews				500	0	0
5. Diverse receipts:						
A. Forfeited lands	418	1	6			
B. Revenues from fiefs in the count's hands	153	13	6			
C. Sales of wheat and other grains	250	1	6			
D. Profits of justice	212	17	6			
TOTAL DIVERSE RECEIPTS:				1034	14	0
TOTAL RECEIPTS:				6687	9	6

Expenses:

```
1.  Garrison payments:
    A. Salaries of the men       1225   2   6
    B. Reinforcements for the
       garrisons                   57  15   0
    C. Summer clothing             18   2   6
              TOTAL:                              1301   0   0
2.  Garrisons of forfeited lands:
    A. La Roche-sur-Yon            47   0   0
    B. Tiffauges                  119   5   0
    C. Civray                      40   0   0
              TOTAL:                               206   5   0
3.  Alms and feudal dues[1]                        247   0   0
4.  Public works                                   129  10   0
5.  Minor expenses                                 106   9   9
6.  Wages of the bailli                             96   0   0
              TOTAL EXPENSES:                      2086   4   9

BALANCE DUE TO THE COUNT:                          4601   4   9
```

[1] Alms and feudal dues are not seperable for this term because of manuscript illegibility.

ASCENSION, 1247

DOMAIN OF THE COUNT OF POITIERS

Item	Revenue		
	l.	s.	d.
1. Provostship of Poitiers	100	0	0
2. Provostship of Niort	113	6	8
3. Provostship of Benon	80	0	0
4. Provostship of La Rochelle	533	6	8
5. Provostship of Saint-Jean-d'Angély	43	6	8
6. Provostship of Fontenay-le-Comte	66	13	4
7. Pierre de Soonay for the fief of Affre	26	13	4
8. Pierre Bertin for the fief of G. d'Allemagne	33	6	8
9. Sale of 323 arpents in Moulière	147	15	10
10. Sale of 124 arpents in the same forest	56	16	8
11. Hamenon de la Roche for his wife's relief	40	0	0
12. Profits from the forest of Benon	12	0	0
TOTAL:	1253	5	10
MANUSCRIPT TOTAL:	1253	5	10

DOMAIN OF COUNT HUGH DE LA MARCHE

Item	Revenue		
	l.	s.	d.
1. Land of Count Hugh de La Marche at Poitiers	35	0	0
2. Provostship of Montreuil	126	13	4
3. Farm of Cherveux	33	6	8
4. Farm of Sanxay	13	6	8
5. Provostship of Frontenay	83	6	8
6. Farm of Coulons	13	6	8
7. Farm of Prahecq	73	6	8
8. Grand fief of Aunis	416	13	4
9. Provostship of Tonnay-Boutonne	50	0	0
10. Fief of La Croix-Comtesse	26	13	4
11. Provostship of Saintes and fief of Ramegot and Ramiet	133	6	8
12. Customary dues from Château-Neuf, Saint-Gemme, and Favaux	20	0	0
13. Pasturage rights in the forest of Baconais	40	0	0
14. Forest duties in Baconais	6	18	0
15. Profits of justice from Baconais	18	12	0
16. Ripuarian rights at Saint-Jean-d'Angély	2	6	8
17. Farm of the fief of Graves	7	10	0
18. Profits from the mills on the bridge of Saintes	7	0	0
19. Minor customary revenues	3	5	4
20. Sale in the forest of Montreuil	71	18	10
21. Sale in the forest of Vaumaingot	24	8	10
22. Dead wood sold to the glassmakers in the forest of Montreuil	7	6	8
23. From the forest and warren of Tonnay-Boutonne	20	0	0
24. From the woods at Grateloup	3	0	0
25. From the woods at La Croix-Comtesse	18	6	8
TOTAL:	1255	13	0
MANUSCRIPT TOTAL:	1255	13	0

ASCENSION, 1247

GARRISON PAYMENTS

(TERM: 135 DAYS)

Item	Per Diem			Total		
	l.	s.	d.	l.	s.	d.
1. Poitiers		12	1	81	11	3
2. Saint-Maixent		16	8	112	10	0
3. Niort	1	9	2	196	17	6
4. Benon		12	11	87	3	9
5. La Rochelle	1	19	0	263	5	0
6. Saint-Jean-d'Angély		7	9	52	6	3
7. Saintes (castle)	2	0	7	273	18	9
8. Saintes (bridge)		2	1	14	1	3
9. Fontenay-le-Comte		6	0	40	10	0
10. Sergeant Pozole		7	3	48	18	9
11. Robert de Gondreville		4	0	27	0	0
12. Robert (in Montreuil)		4	0	27	0	0
TOTAL:	9	1	6	1225	2	6

Giraud Ebert (365 days) (June 24, 1246-June 24, 1247)		3	0	54	15	0
The smith at the castle of Saintes (36 days) (Feb. 9-Mar. 17, 1247)		1	8	3	0	0
Summer clothing for the garrisons				18	2	6
FINAL TOTAL:				1301	0	0
MANUSCRIPT TOTAL:				1301	1	8

GARRISON PAYMENTS IN FORFEITED LANDS

Item	Per Diem		Total		
	l. s. d.		l. s. d.		
La Roche-sur-Yon:					
1. Garrison payments not yet farmed out (21 days) (Feb. 9-Mar. 2, 1247)	6 8		7	0	0
2. First third of the farm payment			40	0	0
TOTAL:			47	0	0
Tiffauges:					
Garrison of the castle of Tiffauges (135 days) (Feb. 9-June 24, 1247)	17 8		119	5	0
Civray:					
First third of the farm payment for the castle at Civray			40	0	0
TOTAL GARRISON:			206	5	0
MANUSCRIPT TOTAL:			206	5	0

ALL SAINTS' DAY, 1247

SUMMARY ACCOUNT OF THE GENERAL FUND:

ORIGINAL MANUSCRIPT TOTALS

Item	Subtotal			Total		
	l.	s.	d.	l.	s.	d.
Receipts:						
1. Forfeited baronies	1722	19	9			
2. Reliefs	4600	0	0			
3. Redemptions of for- feited lands	768	0	0			
4. Assessment of the Jews	500	0	0			
5. Domain of Count Alphonse	1156	16	0			
6. Domain of Hugh de La Marche	1614	2	2			
7. Forfeited lands	676	10	0			
8. Castleward at Tiffauges	40	0	0			
9. Profits of justice	240	0	0			
TOTAL RECEIPTS:				11,318	7	11
Receipts separated and repeated:						
1. Forfeited baronies	1722	19	9			
2. Reliefs	4600	0	0			
3. Redemption of for- feited lands	768	0	0			
4. Assessment of the Jews	500	0	0			
TOTAL:				7590	19	9
REMAINING RECEIPTS:				3727	8	2
MANUSCRIPT TOTAL:				3726	14	0
Expenses:						
1. Garrison payments	1372	5	8			
2. Alms and feudal dues	838	3	5			
3. Public works	507	5	4			
4. Minor expenses	51	10	3			
5. Wages of the bailli	176	0	0			
TOTAL EXPENSES:				2945	4	3
MANUSCRIPT TOTAL:				2845	4	3
BALANCE DUE TO THE COUNT:				782	3	11
MANUSCRIPT BALANCE:				781	9	9

ALL SAINTS' DAY, 1247

SUMMARY ACCOUNT OF THE GENERAL FUND:

REORGANIZED TOTALS

Item	Subtotal			Total		
	l.	s.	d.	l.	s.	d..
Receipts:						
1. Domain receipts:						
A. Domain of Count Alphonse	1156	16	0			
B. Domain of Hugh de La						
Marche	1614	2	2			
TOTAL DOMAIN RECIEPTS:				2770	18	2
2. Forfeited baronies				1722	11	9
3. Reliefs				4600	0	0
4. Redemptions of forfeited						
lands				768	0	0
5. Assessment of the Jews				500	0	0
6. Diverse receipts:						
A. Forfeited lands	676	0	0			
B. Castleward at Tiffauges	40	0	0			
C. Profits of justice	240	0	0			
TOTAL DIVERSE RECEIPTS:				956	0	0
TOTAL RECEIPTS:				11,317	9	11
Expenses:						
1. Garrison payments:						
A. Salaries of the men	1251	5	4			
B. Payments at Tiffauges	121	0	4			
TOTAL:				1372	5	8
2. Alms and feudal dues:						
A. Feudal dues	736	13	4			
B. Alms	101	9	8			
TOTAL:				838	3	0
3. Public works				507	5	4
4. Minor expenses				51	10	3
5. Wages of the <u>bailli</u>				176	0	0
TOTAL EXPENSES:				2945	4	3
BALANCE DUE TO THE COUNT:				8372	5	8

ALL SAINTS' DAY, 1247

DOMAIN OF THE COUNT OF POITIERS

Item	Revenue		
	l.	s.	d.
1. Provostship of Poitiers	100	0	0
2. Provostship of Niort	113	6	0
3. Provostship of Benon	80	0	0
4. Provostship of La Rochelle	533	6	8
5. Provostship of Saint-Jean-d'Angély	43	6	8
6. Provostship of Fontenay-le-Comte	66	13	4
7. Pierre de Soonay for the fief of Affre	26	13	4
8. Pierre Bertin for the fief of G. d'Allemagne	33	6	8
9. Hamenon de la Roche for his wife's relief	40	0	0
10. Lodging rights at Anais	5	0	0
11. Aids at Boece	60	0	0
12. Relief of the lands of Guy le Senechal	33	6	8
13. Rents of new settlers in Moulière	1	16	0
14. Profits from the forest of Moulière	10	0	0
15. Profits from the forest of Benon	10	0	0
TOTAL:	1156	16	0
MANUSCRIPT TOTAL:	1156	16	0

DOMAIN OF COUNT HUGH DE LA MARCHE

Item	Revenue		
	l.	s.	d.
1. Land of Count Hugh de La Marche at Poitiers	35	0	0
2. Provostship of Montreuil	126	13	4
3. Fief of Cherveux	33	6	8
4. Fief of Sanxay	13	6	8
5. Provostship of Frontenay	83	6	8
6. Provostship of Prahecq	73	6	8
7. Provostship of Coulons	13	6	8
8. Grand fief of Aunis	416	13	4
9. Provostship of Tonnay-Boutonne	50	0	0
10. Fief of Graves	7	10	0
11. Aids from the fief of Hericon	3	10	0
12. Fief of La Croix-Comtesse	26	13	4
13. Provostship of Saintes and fief of Ramegot	133	6	8
14. Fief of the Lady of Contor	11	12	0
15. Rents aroung La Vergne	1	2	6
16. Sale of grain from the district of La Vergne	3	3	0
17. Sale of hay from the district of La Vergne		2	0
18. For the extension of the forest farm at Baconais	10	6	0
19. Forest dues at Baconais[1]	40	0	0
20. Profits from the forest of Baconais	13	10	0
21. Farm of minor customs from Saint-Gemme, Favaux, and Château-Neuf	20	0	0
22. River dues from Saint-Jean-d'Angély	3	0	0
23. Minor ripuarian rights at Marennes	3	6	0
24.	1	1	6
25. Aids of the abbess of Saintes	175	0	0
26. Aids of Saint-Anais at the feast of St. John	7	0	0
27. Aids of Saint-Anais at the feast of St. Michael	50	0	0
28. Relief of the lands of Arnould Cougis	8	0	0
29. Relief of Arnould Jolain	7	0	0
30. Relief of Guillaume de Muron	2	0	0
31. Relief of the Lady of Dompierre by P. Giraud	40	0	0
32. The seigneur of Montocq for his wife's relief	30	0	0

33. The goods of a murderer in Montreuil	5	7	0
34. Revenue from the lands of Jocelin de Lazay to the count for failure of service	3	8	0
35. Guillaume de Saint-Gelais for horse service[2]	3	0	0
36. Grain sold from taxed fields	1	3	2
37. Sale in the forest of Montreuil	71	18	10
38. Sale in the woods of Vaumaingot	24	8	10
39. Dead woodsold to the glassmakers	7	6	8
40. Sale of wood in the warren of Tonnay-Boutonne	20	0	0
41. Sale of wood at Grateloup	3	0	0
42. Sale of wood at La Croix-Comtesse	18	6	8
43. Rabbits sold by the provost of Montreuil	14	0	0
TOTAL:	1614	2	2

MANUSCRIPT TOTAL: 1614 2 2

[1]Entries for 19 and 20 are effaced in the manuscript. The value of the farm was determined from the preceding term and the extra payment was computed by substraction from the total in the manuscript.

[2]"...pro roncino de servicio de feodo..," ms. 133v, Bardonnet, p. 176. Cf. F. L. Ganshof, Feudalism (New York, 1961), p. 91.

ALL SAINTS' DAY, 1247

GARRISON PAYMENTS

(TERM: 137 DAYS)

Item	Per Diem			Total		
	l.	s.	d.	l.	s.	d.
1. Poitiers		12	1	82	15	5
2. Saint-Maixent		16	8	114	3	4
3. Niort	1	9	2	199	15	10
4. Benon		12	11	88	9	7
5. La Rochelle	1	19	0	267	3	0
6. Saint-Jean-d'Angély		7	9	53	1	9
7. Saintes (castle)	1	18	9	265	8	9
8. Saintes (bridge)		2	1	14	5	5
9. Fontenay-le-Comte		6	0	41	2	0
10. Sergeant Pozole		7	3	49	13	3
11. Robert (in Montreuil)		4	0	27	8	0
12. Giraud Ebert		3	0	20	11	0
13. Robert de Gondreville		4	0	27	8	0
TOTAL:	9	2	8	1251	5	4
MANUSCRIPT TOTAL:				1251	5	4
Garrison at Tiffauges		17	8	121	0	4
FINAL TOTAL:				1372	5	8
MANUSCRIPT TOTAL:				1372	5	8

CANDLEMAS, 1247

SUMMARY ACCOUNT OF THE GENERAL FUND:

ORIGINAL MANUSCRIPT TOTALS

Item	Subtotal			Total		
	l.	s.	d.	l.	s.	d.

Receipts:

1.	Mint revenues	1500	0	0			
2.	Forfeited baronies	1164	6	6			
3.	Reliefs	200	0	0			
4.	Redemptions of forfeited lands	250	0	0			
5.	Assessment of the Jews	500	0	0			
6.	Domain ofCount Alphonse	1258	14	6			
7.	Domain of Hugh de La Marche	1360	1	4			
8.	Forfeited lands	441	8	10			
9.	Castleward at Tiffauges	40	0	0			
10.	Castleward outside the provostships	35	0	0			
11.	Profits of justice	273	10	0			
	TOTAL RECEIPTS:				7023	1	2

Receipts separated and repeated:

1.	Mint revenues	1500	0	0			
2.	Forfeited baronies	1164	6	6			
3.	Reliefs	200	0	0			
4.	Redemptions of forfeited lands	250	0	0			
5.	Assessment of the Jews	500	0	0			
	TOTAL:				3614	6	6
	REMAINING RECEIPTS:				3408	14	8
	MANUSCRIPT TOTAL:				3408	14	8

Expenses:

.1.	Garrison payments	1069	18	0
2.	Alms and feudal dues	421	10	0
3.	Public works	192	16	10
4.	Minor expenses	86	13	0
5.	Wages of the bailli	93	0	0

TOTAL EXPENSES: 1863 17 10

MANUSCRIPT TOTAL: 1863 17 10

BALANCE DUE TO THE COUNT: 1544 16 10

MANUSCRIPT BALANCE: 1544 16 10

CANDLEMAS, 1247

SUMMARY ACCOUNT OF THE GENERAL FUND:

REORGANIZED TOTALS

Item	Subtotal			Total		
	l.	s.	d.	l.	s.	d.

Receipts:

1. Domain receipts:
   A. Domain of Count Alphonse 1258 14 6
   B. Domain of Hugh de La
      Marche   1361 1 4
      TOTAL DOMAIN RECEIPTS: 2619 15 10
2. Mint revenues   1500 0 0
3. Forfeited baronies   1164 6 6
4. Reliefs   200 0 0
5. Redemptions of forfeited lands   250 0 0
6. Assessment of the Jews   500 0 0
7. Diverse receipts:
   A. Forfeited lands   441 18 10
   B. Castleward at Tiffauges 40 0 0
   C. Castleward outside the
      provostships   35 0 0
   D. Profits of justice   273 10 0
      TOTAL DIVERSE RECEIPTS: 790 8 10

      TOTAL RECEIPTS: 7024 11 2

```
Expenses:

1. Garrison payments:
   A. Salaries of the men        849  8  0
   B. Master Richard Turiot        5  4  6
   C. Clothing                   133  2  8
   D. Payments at Tiffauges       82  3  0
      TOTAL:                                  1069 18  2
2. Alms and feudal dues
   A. Feudal dues                149 13  4
   B. Alms                       271 16  8
      TOTAL:                                   421 10  0
3. Public works                                191 16 10
4. Minor expenses                               86 13  0
5. Wages of the bailli                          93  0  0
      TOTAL EXPENSES:                         1862 18  0

BALANCE DUE TO THE COUNT:                     5161 13  2
```

CANDLEMAS, 1247

DOMAIN OF THE COUNT OF POITIERS

Item	Revenue		
	l.	s.	d.
1. Provostship of Poitiers (not farmed)	51	2	0
2. Provostship of Niort	113	6	8
3. Provostship of Benon	80	0	0
4. Provostship of La Rochelle	500	0	0
5. Provostship of Saint-Jean-d'Angély	43	6	8
6. Provostship of Fontenay-le-Comte	60	0	0
7. Sale of 323 arpents in the forest of Moulière	147	15	10
8. Sale of 124 arpents in the forest of Moulière	56	16	8
9. Farm of ardannes	3	6	8
10. Castleward at Fontenay-le-Comte	6	0	0
11. Geoffroy Volsard for pleas at Fontenay-le-Comte	15	0	0
12. Relief of the Lady of Barnagot	15	0	0
13. Hugh de Jarria for his relief	10	0	0
14. Hugh de Jarria for the fine of his wardship	30	0	0
15. Relief for the lands of Guy le Senechal	33	6	8
16. Sale in the forest of Benon	86	13	4
17. Debt of Gautier de Cortean	7	0	0
TOTAL:	1258	14	6
MANUSCRIPT TOTAL:	1258	14	6

DOMAIN OF COUNT HUGH DE LA MARCHE

Item	Revenue

		l.	s.	d.
1.	Provostship of Montreuil	126	13	4
2.	Fief of Cherveux	33	6	8
3.	Provostship of Sanxay	13	6	8
4.	Provostship of Frontenay	83	6	8
5.	Provostship of Prahecq	73	6	8
6.	Farm of Coulons	13	6	8
7.	Grand fief of Aunis	434	6	8
8.	Provostship of Tonnay-Boutonne	50	0	0
9.	Fief of Hericon for minor customs	1	11	4
10.	Fief of La Croix-Comtesse	26	13	4
11.	Provostship of Saintes and fied of Romegot	133	6	8
12.	Farm of minor customs from Saint-Gemme, Favaux, and Château-Neuf	20	0	0
13.	River dues at Saint-Jean-d'Angély	3	0	0
14.	Profits from the forest of Baconais	5	0	0
15.	Rabbits sold from the warren of Saintes	30	0	0
16.	Minor ripuarian rights	1	13	4
17.	Dues for keeping hens at La Vergne (new)	1	6	8
18.	Dues for keeping hens at La Vergne		7	4
19.	The mille at La Vergne	1	5	0
20.	Sale in the forest of Montreuil	71	18	10
21.	Sale in the woods of Vaumaingot	24	8	10
22.	Dead wood sold to the glassmakers	7	6	8
23.	Sale in the forest of Baconais	164	3	4
24.	Sale of wood at La Croix-Comtesse	18	6	8
25.	Sale of wood at the warren of Tonnay-Boutonne	20	0	0
26.	Sale of wood at Hericon	3	0	0
	TOTAL:	1361	t	4
	MANUSCRIPT TOTAL:	1361	1	4

CANDLEMAS, 1247

GARRISON PAYMENTS

(TERM: 93 DAYS)

Item	Per Diem			Total		
	l.	s.	d.	l.	s.	d.
1. Poitiers		12	1	56	3	9
2. Saint-Maixent		16	8	77	10	0
3. Niort	1	9	2	135	12	6
4. Benon		12	11	60	1	3
5. La Rochelle	1	19	0	181	7	0
6. Saint-Jean-d'Angély		7	9	36	0	9
7. Saintes (castle)	1	18	9	180	3	9
8. Saintes (bridge)		2	1	9	13	9
9. Fontenay-le-Comte		6	0	27	18	0
10. Sergeant Pozole		7	3	33	14	3
11. Robert (in Montreuil)		4	0	18	12	0
12. Robert de Gondreville		4	0	18	12	0
13. Giraud d'Ebert		3	0	13	19	0
TOTAL:	9	2	8	849	8	0
MANUSCRIPT TOTAL:				849	8	0

Wages of Master Richard Turiot
        (57 days)(June 24-Aug. 20,
        1247)   1 10   5   4 6
Clothing for the garrisons   133   2 8
Payments at Tiffauges (93 days)
        (Nov. 8, 1247-Feb. 9,
        1248)   17 8   82   3 0

        FINAL TOTAL: 1069 18 2

        MANUSCRIPT TOTAL: 1069 18 0

ASCENSION, 1248

SUMMARY ACCOUNT OF THE GENERAL FUND:

ORIGINAL MANUSCRIPT TOTALS

Item	Subtotal			Total		
	l.	s.	d.	l.	s.	d.

Receipts:

1.	Forfeited baronies	771	8	1			
2.	Redemptions of forfeited lands	750	0	0			
3.	Assessment of the Jews	500	0	0			
4.	Domain of Count Alphonse	1289	14	10			
5.	Domain of Hugh de La Marche	1359	4	0			
6.	Forfeited lands	419	18	4			
7.	Castleward at Tiffauges	40	0	0			
8.	Profits of justice	85	0	0			
	TOTAL RECEIPTS:				5215	5	3

Receipts separated and repeated:

1.	Forfeited baronies	771	8	1			
2.	Redemptions of forfeited lands	750	0	0			
3.	Assessment of the Jews	500	0	0			
	TOTAL:				2021	8	1
	REMAINING RECEIPTS:				3193	17	2
	MANUSCRIPT TOTAL:				3193	17	2

Expenses:

1.	Garrison payments	1441	9	11
2.	Alms and feudal dues	250	0	0
3.	Public works	560	6	11
4.	Minor expenses	275	2	3
5.	Wages of the <u>bailli</u>	116	0	0

```
        TOTAL EXPENSES:              2642 19  1

        MANUSCRIPT TOTAL:           2642 19  1

BALANCE DUE TO THE COUNT:            550 18  1

MANUSCRIPT BALANCE:                  539 18  1
```

SUMMARY ACCOUNT OF THE GENERAL FUND:

REORGANIZED TOTALS

Item	Subtotal			Total		
	l.	s.	d.	l.	s.	d.
Receipts:						
1. Domain receipts:						
A. Domain of Count Alphonse	1289	14	10			
B. Domain of Hugh de La Marche	1359	4	0			
TOTAL DOMAIN RECEIPTS:				2648	18	10
2. Forfeited baronies				771	8	1
3. Redemptions of forfeited lands				750	0	0
4. Assessment of the Jews				500	0	0
5. Diverse receipts:						
A. Forfeited lands	420	12	1			
B. Castleward at Tiffauges	40	0	0			
C. Profits of justice	82	0	0			
TOTAL DIVERSE RECEIPTS:				542	12	1
TOTAL RECEIPTS:				5212	19	0
Expenses:						
1. Garrison payments:						
A. Salaries of the men	1192	16	8			
B. Supplementary wages (outside regular garrisons)	115	19	2			
C. Payments at Tiffauges	111	6	0			
D. Summer clothing	22	10	0			
TOTAL:				1442	11	10
2. Alms and feudal dues						
A. Feudal dues	146	13	4			
B. Alms	101	17	8			
TOTAL:				248	11	0
3. Public works				571	8	9
4. Minor expenses				285	0	3
5. Wages of the bailli				116	0	0
TOTAL EXPENSES:				2663	11	10
BALANCE DUE TO THE COUNT:				2549	7	2

DOMAIN OF THE COUNT OF POITIERS

Item	Revenue		
	l.	s.	d.
1. Provostship of Poitiers	100	9	4
2. Provostship of Niort	113	6	8
3. Provostship of Benon	80	0	0
4. Provostship of La Rochelle	500	0	0
5. Provostship of Saint-Jean-d'Angély[1]	43	6	8
6. Provostship of Fontenay-le-Comte	60	0	0
7. Farm of the fief of Ardannes	3	6	8
8. Relief of the Lady of Barnagot	15	0	0
9. Relief of the lands of Guy le Senechal	33	6	8
10. Relief of the lands and wardship of Hugh de Jarria	30	0	0
11. Sale of 323 arpents in the forest of Moulière	147	15	10
12. Sale of 124 arpents in the forest of Moulière	56	16	8
13. Aimeri d'Oleron for pleas	1	5	0
14. Pleas from P. Constantin	1	0	0
15. Profits from the use of the forest of Benon	17	8	0
16. Sale in the forest of Benon	86	13	4
TOTAL:	1289	14	10
MANUSCRIPT TOTAL:	1289	14	10

[1]The scribe and Bardonnet erred on this entry. The scribe wrote "VIIII d." while intending "VIII" as is the case throughout the accounting terms. Bardonnet misread "XLIII l." for "XIIIII."

DOMAIN OF COUNT HUGH DE LA MARCHE

Item	Revenue		
	l.	s.	d.
1. Provostship of Montreuil	126	13	4
2. Fief of Cherveux	33	6	8
3. Provostship of Sanxay	13	6	8
4. Provostship of Frontenay	83	6	8
5. Provostship of Prahecq	73	6	8
6. Farm of Coulons	13	6	8
7. Grand fief of Aunis	433	6	8
8. Provostship of Tonnay-Boutonne	50	0	0
9. Fief of La Croix-Comtesse	26	13	4
10. Provostship of Saintes and fief of Ramegot	133	6	8
11. Farm of minor customs from Saint-Gemme, Favaux, and Château-Neuf	20	0	0
12. River dues at Saint-Jean-d'Angély	3	0	0
13. Dues for the maintenance of animals near La Vergne	6	18	0
14. Forest dues at Baconais	40	0	0
15. Profits from the forest of Baconais	7	17	0
16. Minor river dues		12	0
17. Salt dues		16	0
18. Sale in the forest of Montreuil	71	18	10
19. Sale of wood at Vaumaingot	24	8	10
20. Sale of dead wood to the glassmakers	7	6	8
21. Sale in the forest of Baconais	164	3	4
22. Sale of wood at Hericon	3	0	0
23. Sale of wood at Cherveux	15	0	0
24. Fief of Garnia	7	10	0
TOTAL:	1359	4	0
MANUSCRIPT TOTAL:	1359	4	0

ASCENSION, 1248

GARRISON PAYMENTS

(TERM: 136 DAYS)

Item	Per Diem			Total		
	l.	s.	d.	l.	s.	d.
1. Poitiers		12	1	82	3	4
2. Saint-Maixent		16	8	113	6	8
3. Niort	1	9	2	198	6	8
4. Benon		12	11	87	16	8
5. La Rochelle	1	19	0	265	4	0
6. Saint-Jean-d'Angély		7	9	52	14	0
7. Saintes (castle)	1	18	9	263	10	0
8. Saintes (bridge)		2	1	14	3	4
9. Fontenay-le-Comte		6	0	40	16	0
10. Robert (in Montreuil)		4	0	27	4	0
11. Robert (in Baconais)		4	0	27	4	0
12. Giraud d'Ebert		3	0	20	8	0
TOTAL:	8	15	5	1192	16	8
MANUSCRIPT TOTAL:				1192	16	8

Sergeant Pozole (109 days)						
(Feb. 9-May 28, 1248)		7	3	39	10	3
Clothing for Sergeant Pozole[1]				3	2	6
The smith at Saintes (107 days)						
(Mar. 9-June 24, 1248)		1	10	9	16	2
Guillaume de Perdillan (12 days)		6	3	3	15	0
Guillaume de Perdillan (15 days)		3	0	2	5	0
Guillaume de Perdillan (23 days)		6	3	7	3	9
Guillaume de Perdillan (21 days)						
(April 20-May 11, 1248)		3	0	3	3	0
Guillaume de Perdillan (2 days)		3	3		6	6
Nicholas de Perdillan and Pierre						
d'Arpillan (36 days)		5	0	10	16	0
Nicholas de Perdillan and Pierre						
d'Arpillan (6 days)		6	0	1	16	0
Nicholas de Perdillan for expenses				1	5	0
Nicholas and Pierre (44 days)						
(May 11-June 14, 1248)		15	0	33	0	0
Summer clothing				22	10	0
Tiffauges (126 days)						
(Feb. 9-June 14, 1248)		17	8	111	6	0
FINAL TOTAL:				1442	11	10
MANUSCRIPT TOTAL:				1441	9	11

[1]This entry was conbined with the preceding one in the manuscript.

ALL SAINTS' DAY, 1248

SUMMARY ACCOUNT OF THE GENERAL FUND:

ORIGINAL MANUSCRIPT TOTALS

Item	Subtotal			Total		
	l.	s.	d.	l.	s.	d.

Receipts:

1.	Forfeited baronies	668	18	11			
2.	Redemptions of forfeited lands	294	0	0			
3.	Reliefs	2000	0	0			
4.	Fines for mortmain	1413	6	8			
5.	Commutation of two payments by Hugh Chace-porc	22	0	0			
6.	Domain of Count Alphonse	994	2	8			
7.	Domain of Hugh de La Marche	1455	6	4			
8.	Forfeited lands	583	2	5			
9.	Sale of grain	69	11	6			
10.	Castleward at Tiffauges	40	0	0			
11.	Fine of G. Raymon	100	0	0			
12.	Profits of justice	206	0	0			
	TOTAL RECEIPTS:				7846	8	6

Receipts separated and repeated:

1.	Forfeited bariones	668	18	11			
2.	Redemptions of forfeited lands	294	0	0			
3.	Reliefs	2000	0	0			
4.	Fines for mortmain	1413	6	8			
5.	Commutation of two payments by Hugh Chace-porc	22	0	0			
	TOTAL:				4398	5	7
	REMAINING RECEIPTS:				3448	2	11
	MANUSCRIPT TOTAL:				3448	2	11

Expenses:

1.	Garrison payments	1579	4	0
2.	Alms and feudal dues	867	17	0
3.	Public works	928	2	1
4.	Minor expenses	136	3	4
5.	Wages of the <u>bailli</u>	166	0	0

TOTAL EXPENSES: 3677   6   5

BALANCE DUE TO THE COUNT: -229   3   6
MANUSCRIPT BALANCE: -229   3   6

ALL SAINTS' DAY, 1248

SUMMARY ACCOUNT OF THE GENERAL FUND:

REORGANIZED TOTALS

Item	Subtotal			Total		
	l.	s.	d.	l.	s.	d.

Receipts:

1. Domain receipts:
  A. Domain of Count Alphonse

	Subtotal			Total		
1. Domain receipts:						
A. Domain of Count Alphonse	994	2	8			
B. Domain of Hugh de La Marche	1455	6	4			
TOTAL DOMAIN RECEIPTS:				2449	9	0
2. Forfeited baronies				668	18	11
3. Redemptions of forfeited lands				293	10	0
4. Reliefs				2000	0	0
5. Fines for mortmain				1413	6	8
6. Commutation of two payments by Hugh Chace-porc				22	0	0
7. Diverse receipts:						
A. Forfeited lands	583	13	4			
B. Sale of grain	67	16	6			
C. Castleward at Tiffauges	40	0	0			
D. Fine of G. Raymon	100	0	0			
E. Profits of justice	206	0	0			
TOTAL DIVERSE RECEIPTS:				997	9	10
TOTAL RECEIPTS:				7844	14	5

Expenses:

```
1.  Garrison payments:
    A. Salaries of the men        1279 16   2
    B. Wages not in regular
       garrison payments            68 18   9
    C. Tiffauges                   121  0   4
    D. Vouvent                      94  3   9
       TOTAL:                                1563 19   0
2.  Alms and feudal dues:
    A. Feudal dues                 738  7   4
    B. Alms                        129  9   8
       TOTAL:                                 867 17   0
3.  Public works                                928  2   1
4.  Minor expenses                              136  3   3
5.  Wages of the bailli                         166  0   0
       TOTAL EXPENSES:                         3662  1   4

BALANCE DUE TO THE COUNT:                      4182 13   1
```

ALL SAINTS' DAY, 1248

DOMAIN OF THE COUNT OF POITIERS

Item	Revenue		
	l.	s.	d.
1. Provostship of Poitiers	100	0	0
2. Provostship of Niort	113	6	8
3. Provostship of Benon	73	6	8
4. Provostship of La Rochelle	500	0	0
5. Provostship of Saint-Jean-d'Angély	43	6	8
6. Provostship of Fontenay-le-Comte	60	0	0
7. Farm of the fief of Ardannes	3	6	8
8. Rents for new fields at Moulière	2	5	0
9. Fee for entry into two new farms	2	10	0
10. Rents for newly cleared fields at Benon	8	5	0
11. Value of 96 capons from Benon	2	10	0
12. Profits from the forest of Moulière	9	6	0
13. Profits from the forest of Benon	6	0	0
14. Aids from Boece	60	0	0
15. Lodging rights at Anais	10	0	0
TOTAL:	994	2	8
MANUSCRIPT TOTAL:	994	2	8

DOMAIN OF COUNT HUGH DE LA MARCHE

	Item	Revenue		
		l.	s.	d.
1.	Provostship of Montreuil	120	0	0
2.	Farm of Sanxay	13	6	8
3.	Provostship of Frontenay	83	6	8
4.	Provostship of Prahecq	73	6	8
5.	Farm of Coulons	11	13	4
6.	Grand fief of Aunis	433	6	8
7.	Provostship of Tonnay-Boutonne	50	0	0
8.	Fief of La Croix-Comtesse	26	13	4
9.	Provostship of Saintes and fief of Ramegot	133	6	8
10.	Minor customary revenues from Cherveux	8	6	7
11.	Farm of harvest dues at Favaux and Château-Neuf	23	6	9
12.	Profits from the forest of Baconais	7	6	0
13.	Forest offerings	7	4	0
14.	Forest dues not farmed out	52	10	0
15.	Harvest dues at La Vergne (not farmed out)	4	8	0
16.	Harvest dues farmed to Jean Dimier	6	13	4
17.	River dues	5	7	0
18.	Fief of the Lady of Contor and the Lord of Brou	15	0	0
19.	Sales of grain at La Vergne	4	2	0
20.	Farm of Graves	7	10	0
21.	Fief of Hericon	3	10	0
22.	Aids of the abbess of Saintes	175	0	0
23.	Aids of Saint-Anais at the feast of St. John	7	0	0
24.	Aids of Saint-Anais at the feast of St. Michael	50	0	0
25.	Sale of wood in the forest of Montreuil	71	18	10
26.	Sale of wood at Vaumaingot	24	8	10
27.	Dead wood sold to the glassmakers	11	0	0
28.	Sale of wood at Cherveux	15	0	0
29.	Sale of wood at Frontenay	8	0	0
30.	Jean Marcou, pleas	1	5	0
31.	Jean Marcou, half of horse service[1]	1	10	0
	TOTAL:	1455	6	4
	MANUSCRIPT:	1455	6	4

[1] "...pro dimidio roncino de servicio...," ms. 153v, Bardonnet, p. 219. Cf. Ganshof, p. 91.

ALL SAINTS' DAY, 1248

GARRISON PAYMENTS

(TERM: 137 DAYS)

Item	Subtotal			Total		
	l.	s.	d.	l.	s.	d.
1. Poitiers		12	1	82	15	5
2. Saint-Maixent		16	8	114	3	4
3. Niort	1	9	2	199	15	10
4. Benon		12	11	88	9	7
5. La Rochelle	2	0	3	275	14	3
6. Saint-Jean-d'Angély		7	9	53	1	9
7. Saintes (castle)	2	4	3	303	2	3
8. Saintes (bridge)		2	1	14	5	5
9. Fontenay-le-Comte		6	0	41	2	0
10. Hurtaut (in Montreuil)		3	8	25	2	4
11. Robert (in Baconais)		4	0	27	8	0
12. Giraud d'Ebert		5	0	34	5	0
13. Guy and Gislebert		3	0	20	11	0
TOTAL:	9	6	10	1279	16	2

MANUSCRIPT TOTAL:				1279	16	2
The harnessmakers of Saintes (May 1-June 24, 1248) (54 days)		1	8	4	10	0
Guy and Gislebert (35 days) (May 20-June 24, 1248)		3	0	5	5	0
Master P. Kanoter (35 days) (May 20-June 24, 1248)		1	3	2	3	9
The castellan of Saintes				9	15	0
Tiffauges		17	8	121	0	4
Vouvent		13	9	94	3	9
Wages of five archers (63 days) (Sept. 6-Nov. 8, 1248)		15	0	47	5	0
FINAL TOTAL:				1563	19	0